WORKING IN COMPLEMENTARY
—— AND ——
ALTERNATIVE
MEDICINE

A
Career
Guide

Loulou Brown

**KOGAN
PAGE**

First published in 1994

Apart from any fair dealing for the purposes of research or private study, or criticism or review, as permitted under the Copyright, Designs and Patents Act, 1988, this publication may only be reproduced, stored or transmitted, in any form or by any means, with the prior permission in writing of the publishers, or in the case of reprographic reproduction in accordance with the terms of licences issued by the Copyright Licensing Agency. Enquiries concerning reproduction outside those terms should be sent to the publishers at the undermentioned address:

Kogan Page Limited
120 Pentonville Road
London N1 9JN

© Loulou Brown 1994

British Library Cataloguing in Publication Data

A CIP record for this book is available from the British Library.

ISBN 0-7494-1223-2

Typeset by Saxon Graphics Ltd, Derby
Printed and bound in Great Britain by Clays Ltd, St Ives plc

Contents

Contents

Acknowledgements

While researching and writing this book I have been in contact with a great many people, either on the phone, through books and articles, or directly face to face. Thank you all very much for your help. I particularly want to mention the following.

First, an enormous thank you to Elisabeth Brooke, MNIMH, a herbalist, whose books I have read assiduously and whose ideas and vast knowledge have provided the underpinning for this book. She has read what I have written and her detailed comments and suggested amendments, almost all of which I have incorporated, have made this a very much better book than it would have been without her help. Thank you, too, to Helen Franks, who started me off in the right direction by allowing me to look through her collection of articles relating to holistic medicine and who put me in contact with relevant organisations. In addition, I would like to thank Jenny Boakes, an inspiring teacher of reflexology and Bach Flower Remedies at the City Literary Institute, who imbued me with the enthusiasm for writing the book which has remained with me throughout the last nine months.

I would like to acknowledge and thank the following who have taken the time to talk to me at length and who for the most part have read specific chapters for factual accuracy: James Colton, Chairman, Society of Iridologists; Jenny Crewdson, Certified Rolfer; Chris Devereux, Polarity Therapy practitioner; Helen Fox, Core Group Member, Shiatsu Society; Alf Fowles, Director, Association of Ethical and Professional Hypnotherapists; Jeremy Gilbey BSc (Hons), DO, MRO, registered Osteopath; Joseph Goodman, Chairman, Council of Acupuncture; Stephen Gordon, Director, Council for Complementary and Alternative Medicine; Major Gordon Smith of the Confederation of Radionic and Radiesthesic Organisations; Nicola M Hall, Director, Bayly

School of Reflexology; Judy Howard, Consultant, The Dr Edward Bach Centre; Hilary King, MSTAT, a teacher of the Alexander Technique; Maureen Li, MIIR, reflexologist; Michael McIntyre, President of the National Institute of Medical Herbalists, Judith Marshall, Registrar, British College of Naturopathy and Osteopathy; Glynn Macdonald, Chairperson of the Society of Teachers of the Alexander Technique; Rhona Myers, LCH, homoeopath; Nicole Perez, MIFA, Director of the School of Holistic Aromatherapy; Professor Patrick Pietroni, FRCGP, MRCP, DCH, Founder Member and Former Chairman of the British Holistic Medical Association; Donald Pike, Director, McTimoney Chiropractic School; Enid Segall, Secretary General of the British Homoeopathic Association; Dr John Sketchley, Education Adviser, General Council and Register of Osteopaths; Janet Southall of the British Wheel of Yoga; Eli Stern, LCH, homoeopath; Howard Sun, Director, Living Colour; Francis Treuherz, Director, Society of Homoeopaths; Mrs H L Waters, Administrator, McTimoney Chiropractic; Zita West, MTAcS, acupuncture practitioner.

Naturally, the responsibility for the final text is mine.

Loulou Brown
London, May 1994

Foreword

By Professor Patrick Pietroni, FRCGP, MRCP, DCH, Founder Member and Former Chairman of the British Holistic Medical Association.

With the growing interest in alternative and complementary therapies has come the realisation of the need for proper evaluation and training. As with all new clinical endeavours, the first requirement is to ask the question, 'What are we talking about?' This is not an easy question to answer because alternative therapies are by definition 'everything that is not covered at a Western medical school'. This definition includes everything from Acupuncture to Zen meditation. Clearly, the only link between some alternative therapies is what they are not, rather than what they are. For conventionally trained practitioners and, of equal importance, patients/clients, it is very necessary to have a practical guide to these therapies and, more importantly, an outline of the training involved. This book is therefore very timely, coming as it does a year after the Osteopaths Bill was passed by Parliament establishing for the first time in the UK the statutory requirements for one area of complementary therapy. Other Bills are in the pipe-line covering some of the major clinical activities and European legislation will eventually ensure that the public is protected from untrained and unacceptable alternative therapies.

The synthesis of conventional and complementary medicine is long overdue and it is important that both groups of practitioners recognise the strengths and weaknesses in both systems. The concepts involved in 'holistic practice' are as valid whether practised by a conventional doctor or a traditional Chinese acupuncturist.

The future lies in the proper training of all practitioners and this book goes a long way to fill the gap within the field of complementary therapies.

July 1994

1

Introduction

The British Medical Association (BMA) has recently suggested that anyone, whether doctor or patient, who seeks the help of non-conventional therapists should ask a number of questions. Are they registered with a professional organisation? If so, does this have a public register, code of practice, effective disciplinary procedures and sanctions? What qualifications do the therapists hold? What training do they have, and how long have they been practising?

This book hopes to answer some of these questions. It has been written specifically for people who are interested in complementary and alternative medicine and who are thinking of taking a training course in one of the many therapies with a view to subsequently practising in the field. However, the book is also relevant to those who might be associated with conventional medicine, and others who simply want to know more about therapies that are becoming increasingly popular but are still not understood. Each therapy discussed is first defined and its principles listed. A short history is then provided, followed by an account of the situation today. The conditions treated are listed and treatment is discussed at some length. Detailed lists of training schools, the training supplied and professional associations are set out. Every effort has been made to ensure that the most reputable organisations are included.

Why 'Complementary and Alternative' Medicine?

Before the mid-1960s there was no generic term that covered therapies which were not part of conventional medicine as currently practised in the UK. At that time, however, there was a sudden growth in new therapies originating from both the East (for example, acupuncture from China and Shiatsu from Japan) and the West (osteopathy and chiropractic from the USA). From the mid-1960s to around the mid-1970s, these were collectively derided as 'fringe' and were labelled 'unconventional' or 'unorthodox'. As they came to be increasingly accepted, however, 'alternative' began to be used as an umbrella term, from about the mid-1970s to around the end of the 1980s. (The BMA's largely hostile report in 1986, which dismissed the interest in complementary and alternative medicine as a 'passing fashion', was entitled Alternative Therapy.) By the beginning of the 1990s, however, the possibly more charitable generic term 'complementary' came into general use. (The BMA's 1993 report was entitled Complementary Medicine, which formally acknowledged complementary and alternative medicine as playing an important role, though the term 'non-conventional therapies' was used throughout the main text.)

It may well be that by the end of the 1990s prefixes will no longer be required. All therapies, whether 'orthodox' or 'unconventional', may simply be termed 'medicine' and be part and parcel of what is provided as medical care as a matter of course, with, it is hoped, patients being allowed the option to choose the type of medicine they prefer.

At present, however, the terms 'complementary' and 'alternative' are both still in current usage and it is suggested that both are indeed relevant. 'Complementary' because there are some therapies, such as osteopathy and chiropractic, which accept many of the underlying principles of, and run in tandem with, conventional medicine. These can be termed complementary without risk of opposition. There are, however, other therapies, such as homoeopathy and herbal medicine, that are fundamentally different in principles and rationale to those of the allopathic tradition, and that are thought to be alternative to conventional medicine both by their adherents and orthodox medical practitioners. In any event, most complementary and alternative therapies claim an underlying holistic philosophical base for their practice.

Holistic Medicine

Holistic medicine treats the whole person. The body is seen as a complete system, with each part, together with the mind and spirit, affecting all other parts. It is not only concerned with the treatment of illness but also with the removal of, or changing, the pre-disposing states, thereby creating better health. As far as illness is concerned, holistic practitioners are not primarily concerned with symptoms but with their underlying cause. They are concerned with why disease – dis-ease – should occur, and with the implication of underlying lack of balance and disharmony.

A holistic practitioner would almost certainly suggest that drugs in controlling symptoms are not dealing with the underlying disturbances. They most probably would also suggest that, not only do drugs prevent elimination of impurities but might actually add to the toxins already prevalent. Surgery is seen to be destroying the natural balance and should only be necessary as a very last resort. It is accepted that a bacterium or virus may trigger an illness, but this implies an already present state or susceptibility of dis-ease in the individual. It is deemed to be the individual with his or her natural healing powers who can throw off illness with the help of a remedy or some form of mechanical treatment. These are seen to be aids, not cures.

Holistic treatment sees the individual's own response as the prime key to healing, rather than the treatment which merely stimulates and supports it. It is therefore presumed necessary for individuals to take an active part in the pursuit of health, by resting, taking exercise, changing eating habits, and perhaps even radically changing the way they lead their lives. Because of the acknowledged importance of the uniqueness of the individual, holistic practitioners do not think that diagnosis can be standardised, and it is often the case that two people who have previously received orthodox treatment and have been diagnosed with the same disease are prescribed different remedies or treatments, according to their individual responses, when they are treated with a holistic therapy. It is important to note that conventional (orthodox) medicine as practised by many doctors can also be holistic. The nature of the therapy does not determine whether or not a practitioner is holistic.

Increasing Interest in Holistic Treatment
Over the last five years in particular, there has been a very great increase in the use of complementary/alternative therapies. There are no exact figures available for the number of consultations, but it may be seen as significant that while one in seven of

the Consumers' Association's 28,000 members surveyed had visited a non-conventional therapist during the previous 12 months in 1985, this figure had increased to one in four in 1991. The increase might be partly because of the increasing demand by patients to be more actively involved in their own health care and to have a range of options; it also might be partly because of the fear of conventional drug treatment and surgery, as well as an awareness of the limitations of allopathic medicine. (In a 1994 report,* 'Added Value: Complementary Therapies and the NHS', p.18, it is stated that one in four patients suffer a deleterious condition as a direct or indirect result of medical treatment, and that one in 10 hospital outpatient admissions represented conditions arising as a result of treatment.) Another reason may be that individuals want more communication and compassion than they actually receive from their GPs and other orthodox medical personnel and have found what they seek from holistic practitioners. (It has been noted that on average holistic therapists spend eight times as long over each consultation than a general practitioner.)

Complementary/Alternative Medicine and the National Health Service (NHS)

The evidence for the wish for complementary/alternative therapies to be provided by the NHS is overwhelming. In 1989, three out of four people surveyed by MORI thought that holistic medicine should be available on the NHS. In 1993 the BMA report[†] suggested that more than 80 per cent of trainee GPs wanted to train in one or more of the complementary/alternative therapies.

---

* Report by Dr Chris Worth, Director of Public Health, West Yorkshire Health Authority.
† *Complementary Medicine: New Approaches to Good Practice*, Oxford University Press.

According to a National Association of Health Authorities and Trusts' (NAHAT) report in 1993, entitled 'Complementary Therapies in the NHS', over 75 per cent of GP fundholders, nearly 75 per cent of Family Health Service Authorities and about 60 per cent of District Health Authorities thought that complementary/alternative therapies should be available on the NHS.

Since April 1992, GPs have been allowed to employ complementary/alternative practitioners in their surgeries, provided the GPs retain clinical responsibility for the patients being treated. The National Consumer Council's 'Guide for the NHS' states that patients in NHS hospitals can request a particular therapy or practitioner, provided the doctor treating the patient is told. Currently, however, there is no statutory provision for patients to seek NHS treatment from complementary or alternative therapists. There are five homoeopathic NHS hospitals and some medical practitioners who also practise holistic therapies, but otherwise this is the only formal link between therapies and the NHS.

The number of complementary/alternative practitioners employed by the NHS is small. There is still a great deal of suspicion on the part of conventional practitioners, partly because of the general lack of knowledge of the various therapies available and partly because of the supposed lack of standard training and written material provided about standards of training, reputable education and training establishments and registering organisations. (The brochures available are often difficult to understand, badly laid out and can be evasive about important details such as fees and the amount of face-to-face tuition provided.) The 1993 BMA Report 'Complementary Medicine' stressed the need for the establishment of a single register with professional standards of training and practice for each of the larger therapies. It is suggested that the provision of umbrella organisations for the smaller therapies may help in this respect.

Money for Training

Training in holistic medicine can be very expensive and every effort has been made to list the current (1994) fees for training courses, together with the minimum total outlay that will be required.

It is worth contacting local authorities to find out whether they provide discretionary grants, though currently this is unlikely owing to the recession and cut-backs in local authority spending. Or you can apply to charities and trusts. Career development loans are available through a partnership arrangement between the Employment Department and three high street banks: Barclays, the Co-Operative and the Clydesdale. You can apply to borrow between £200 and £5,000 to cover up to 80 per cent of course fees, plus the full cost of books, materials and other course expenses. You make no repayments while studying or training, and for three months afterwards. (Further details from Career Development Loans, Freepost, Newcastle upon Tyne X NE85 1BR.)

National Organisations

British Complementary Medicine Association (BCMA)

The BCMA is a consultative organisation representing some 40 organisations in 30 therapies and comprising more than 20,000 practitioners. The Code of Conduct is common to all member organisations. The aim of the BCMA is to encourage the diverse organisations of individual therapies to join together in a single therapy group to act collectively. Its main objectives are to present these groups as a source of information on complementary matters; to facilitate their advancement; to improve standards of practice and management, primarily through education and training; to integrate complementary medicine in the structure of the national healthcare system and to establish a Register of Practitioners. The BCMA is working towards a higher standard of training, through its Education and Training Group, for all therapists for the benefit of practitioner and patient alike.

Council for Complementary and Alternative Medicine (CCAM)

The Council provides a forum for communication and cooperation between professional bodies representing acupuncture, herbal medicine, homoeopathy and osteopathy. The objects of the Council include the establishment and maintenance of a forum for determining standards of education, training, qualification, ethics and discipline for practitioners of complementary and alternative medicine for the protection and benefit of the public. The Council's intention is to promote and maintain the highest standards of training, qualification and treatment in complementary and alternative medicine and to facilitate the dissemination of information relating to it. The individual members of the professional bodies represented within CCAM have all undergone a minimum of three years' training in their chosen therapy.

Institute for Complementary Medicine (ICM)
The ICM was set up to provide the organisational and development infrastructure which is seen as essential for complementary and alternative therapies to move towards a 'higher plane of recognition'. There are a great many organisations, including professional associations and training schools, that have affiliated to the ICM with the purpose of moving towards full academic accreditation by the most appropriate method. The education programme provides a comprehensive framework to include all branches of complementary medicine. The ICM is currently (1994) working towards the foundation of the International College of Complementary Medicine. This will provide courses of a high standard leading to membership of the British Register of Complementary Practitioners, which was set up by the ICM for individual practitioners of complementary medicine to guarantee high standards of training. Around 3,500 people are registered worldwide.

Research Council for Complementary Medicine (RCCM)
The RCCM encourages rigorous research into complementary therapies, higher standards of education and training, and publication of research results. The organisation enables and sponsors research into complementary therapies and promotes greater distribution on research results to bring about wider option in health care. It provides the expertise necessary for research and publishes and disseminates research results. The RCCM bridges the divide between complementary and alternative and conventional practitioners.

2

Acupuncture

Definition and Principles

The word 'acupuncture' means 'pricking with a needle'. It is a treatment that aims to alter the flow of an individual's bodily energy or life force to relieve pain and to restore health.

History

Acupuncture is an ancient therapy and is known to have been practised in China about 3,500 years ago. The first medical textbook on the subject was *Nei Ching Su Wen* (*The Yellow Emperor's Classic of Internal Medicine*), dating from about 400 BC. The roots of acupuncture lie in Traditional Chinese Medicine.

Traditional Chinese Medicine
In Traditional Chinese Medicine (TCM) it is suggested that both health and illness have physical, emotional and spiritual dimensions. It is thought that a life force, *Qi*, circulates in the body along channels known as meridians (*jingluo*) and illness is seen as a pattern of disruption to the *Qi*, never as a disease emanating solely from external sources. Dual flows of energy, known as *yin* and *yang*, are contained within the *Qi* which are at the same time both opposing and complementary forces. Health is dependent upon their being in *tao* (equilibrium). TCM describes the way *Qi* flows in the body, factors which disrupt it, the way to diagnose these disruptions and the way to restore the balance. In conditions of disease the *Qi* is unbalanced and this imbalance has to be treated by piercing the skin at certain points on the meridians with needles to alter the *Qi* balance in the body and restore equilibrium.

Orthodox Western medicine describes many physiological processes in great detail, but says nothing about the life force or why healing responses vary from person to person and from time to time. When dealing with an individual, it looks only for an external cause or agent of one specific disease which it isolates and controls or destroys with drugs or surgery. TCM, however, adopts an holistic approach by taking into account not only the disease symptoms but also age, habits, physical and emotional traits – indeed all aspects of the individual's life and circumstances – to evaluate patterns of disharmony that have arisen and to assess the type and length of treatment required. The symptoms on their own are considered to be merely a part of the syndrome of disharmony making up the whole person.

Traditional Chinese Medicine includes acupuncture, herbal medicine, massage, diet and exercise.

Acupuncture Today

Today in China there are more than 300,000 practitioners of TCM, with 25 colleges training over 6,000 students. The therapy is the established orthodox practice in China, Japan, Korea and Vietnam. In the UK, however, almost all acupuncturists work on a private basis. There are a small number of doctors qualified in orthodox medicine who also practise acupuncture and the therapy is available under the NHS in a very few areas.

Recent clinical trials have established the efficacy of TCM for the treatment of eczema and the dermatology department at Great Ormond Street hospital has recently adopted TCM for the treatment of this skin disease.

In the UK, although the practice and philosophy of acupuncture are based in TCM, many new techniques have been introduced during the past 30 years. For example, stroke patients have successfully been treated by needles inserted into the scalp, and stimulation of selected points in the ear is used to combat the withdrawal symptoms of narcotics, alcohol and nicotine, as well as for counteracting the pangs of hunger during slimming and for treating asthma and tinnitus.

Owing to the increasing popularity of acupuncture in the UK, many people have gone into practice as acupuncturists after attending only very short and inadequate courses in training. At the present time, anyone is entitled to practise acupuncture, regardless of qualification or training. It is therefore very important for anyone wanting treatment to consult only a recognised practitioner, who should have a licence from a local authority to pierce skin, especially because of the overriding need to ensure hygiene and the sterilisation of needles.

Treatment

At the initial session there will be a detailed diagnosis of the illness, which may take up to 90 minutes. Questions will be asked about medical history, symptoms, length of illness, age and lifestyle. The diagnosis will include observations of the tongue, its colour, shape and movement, skin texture and colouring, hair texture, posture and movement, breathing, voice and pulse. Following the diagnosis, a course of treatment will be proposed. A short course averages around 10 sessions, but a severe illness may need up to 100 treatments.

Very fine sterilised needles, hardly thicker than head hair, made of silver or stainless steel, are inserted into the skin for up to 30 minutes. The number of needles varies from one to as many as fifteen. They may be left to achieve their effect, or they may be stimulated by the acupuncturist either manually or electronically. Sometimes no needles are used; the skin may be massaged or gently scratched with the fingers.

A 'Moxa', which is dried *Artemisia vulgaris* (common mugwort), may be burnt in conjunction with, or sometimes in place of, needling. This is known as moxibustion, which is used to promote the energy flow (*Qi*) along the meridians through the body. Acute diseases may be treated daily, while chronic illnesses are usually treated on a weekly basis for a total of about 15–20 treatments. Patients usually start to feel better after four to six treatments. If there is no improvement after six to eight sessions, it may be that the cause of the problem has not been analysed sufficiently.

Acupuncturists may work from home, practise in rented accommodation, join an existing practice, work in a GP's practice or a pain clinic in a local hospital.

Conditions Used For

The very wide range of problems that can be treated by TCM come under the following headings: infectious diseases (such as coughs, colds, diarrhoea); skin diseases (such as acne, psoriasis and eczema); internal diseases (such as back pain, colitis and indigestion); problems related specifically to women (such as menopause, cystitis and uterine prolapse); and addictions (such as alcohol, heroin and nicotine). The therapy is also used as a form of anaesthesia.

The treatment has no side effects, is not addictive and, if used correctly, it is not harmful. However, if needles remain inserted for longer than the body can handle them, there may be granulomatous reactions. Acupuncture does not help conditions where there is a genetic defect (such as muscular dystrophy) or advanced pathological conditions.

Training

The British Acupuncture Accreditation Board

The Board was set up in 1989 as an independent review body to set and monitor standards in acupuncture training, with the aim of ensuring accreditation of competent acupuncture schools. Colleges can apply for candidacy status, which involves meeting certain institutional requirements and criteria. The colleges then carry out a major self-study into their structure and operation in close cooperation with the Board. After successful completion of this work, and subject to the Board's approval of the outcome, colleges may be awarded accredited status. The Board recognises the following purposes of accreditation: to foster high standards of professional education; to encourage institutional self-improvement; to assure the higher education community, the general public and other agencies or organisations that an institution has clearly defined and appropriate objectives; to provide counsel and assistance to developing constitutions and courses; to encourage diversity, experimentation and innovation within the boundaries of generally accepted standards and guidelines of academic quality; and to protect institutions against encroachment.

So far five colleges have been accorded candidacy status. These are the British College of Acupuncture, the College of Traditional Acupuncture, The International College of Oriental Medicine, the London School of Acupuncture and Traditional Chinese Medicine and the Northern College of Acupuncture.

The British College of Acupuncture

The College believes that a detailed knowledge of both Western and Traditional Chinese Medicine is essential to ensure the proper teaching and application of acupuncture. Its brochure states:

> *A knowledge of Western medicine with but a poor knowledge of acupuncture ... means that the treatment of disorders such as asthma, colitis, migraine, arthritis, gynaecological conditions and many others will be beyond the practitioner's capabilities. Knowledge of Traditional Chinese Medicine without the requisite skill in Western clinical diagnosis may mean failure to diagnose a potentially serious situation.*

The college provides a postgraduate training in acupuncture for practitioners already qualified in some branch of orthodox medicine or natural therapeutics.

First year. Devoted to Western medicine, it comprises 14 weekends between October and May; compulsory 16 hours' attendance at the teaching clinic in London, and intensive home study.

Second year. This is concerned with the philosophy and rules of acupuncture and with an in-depth study of the meridians and use and function of the acupuncture points. It comprises one weekend a month between October and June, two days' attendance at the teaching clinic in London, and intensive home study.

Third year. The student is taught to apply the rules already mastered and is introduced to work in the clinic where experience is gained under highly qualified supervision. It comprises one weekend a month between October and June, necessary attendance at the teaching clinic in London (a minimum of 200 hours before qualifying) and intensive home study.

The fees are (for 1993–94): First year £1,600; Second year £1,700 (plus exam fee of £100); Third year £1,950; Total fees £5,350.

The British College of Acupuncture is the official teaching body of the British Acupuncture Association and Register (see p. 25).

The College of Traditional Acupuncture

The licentiate course involves a minimum of three years' training, providing a grounding in the theories and techniques of traditional acupuncture. There are two main stages. The first extends over the initial two years of the course and is mainly theoretical with an emphasis on the diagnostic skills used by the traditional practitioner. The second stage is the third and clinical year with the emphasis on treating patients under supervision, and also includes classroom study and workshops. Students study: anatomy; physiology and pathology of disease (Western medicine); the history of acupuncture; basic theory; meridians and points; traditional diagnosis; treatment and practice. Students are assessed throughout the programme by tutors, tutorial work, written project work, exams and clinical assessment.

To register, applicants should have five GCSEs and two A levels. The fees are currently (1994) about £7,000 for the complete course.

There is an Advanced Training Programme which offers a number of study options, including: advanced material consistent with five-element acupuncture; explorations of Chinese philosophy; a revision of basic clinical skills; advanced interactive work with patients; advanced point location; refinement of intention when needling; practical experience of colour, sound, odour and emotion; information on acupuncture techniques for use in childbirth, anaesthesia and analgesia; guidelines for the treatment of children, pregnant women, the terminally ill and for treating local and acute conditions; and broader aspects of Oriental medicine. The course programme consists of a foundation week, workshops, seminars, project work and individual tutorials.

The cost of each study option varies but currently (1994) in most instances costs £75 for each two-day event.

The College is affiliated to the Traditional Acupuncture Society (see p. 25).

The International College of Oriental Medicine

The College provides a four-year full-time course in acupuncture.

First year. An introduction to Chinese medicine, practical training, including point location, pulse diagnosis and massage, and the study of anatomy in Western medicine.

Second year. The continuing study of Chinese medicine, practical training, including clinical training, supervised pulse diagnosis and *Qi* development, and the integrated study of physiology in Western medicine.

Third year. A more detailed study of Chinese medicine, including differential diagnosis and the treatment of common disorders; practical training, including the treatment of patients and supervised clinics, needle technique and *Qi* development; and an integrated study of pathology of the body systems, including analysis of common disorders, differential diagnosis, orthodox treatment methods and the use of orthodox drugs and their possible side effects.

Fourth year. The specialised study of Chinese medicine, including diet, depression, paediatrics and Chinese pathology, clinical training and practice management and first aid.

The entry requirements are five GCSE passes, including three sciences and English language and two A levels to include human biology, physics or chemistry. The minimum age of entry is 18.

The fees for 1994 are £3,600 for the first year of the course and slightly less for the second and subsequent years, with a total outlay required of around £13,000.

There is also a three-year part-time diploma in acupuncture course for registered acupuncturists. The first and second years consist of eight weekends, with detailed study of TCM, together with the practical applications of acupuncture. The third year includes theories of body diagnosis and practical techniques whereby patients are diagnosed by practitioners. There are written and practical exams.

The current (1994) fees are £1,800 for each year, which is £5,400 for the complete course.

The College is affiliated to the International Register of Oriental Medicine (see p. 25).

The London School of Acupuncture and Traditional Chinese Medicine

There is a four-year full-time diploma course in TCM which offers a professional qualification in acupuncture and Chinese medicine, together with training in core Western medical sciences. The schedule requires, on average, 20 contact hours per week in the academic year, plus an additional 20 hours of home study.

There is also a three-year full-time diploma course in acupuncture and moxibustion, with the same hours as the course listed above. Subjects include: a detailed study of Traditional Chinese Medicine; the *jingluo* system, including the location of acupuncture points and their actions; the disease processes; and specific applications of acupuncture. Research methodology is taught in the third year. The course also includes a thorough grounding in Western medical science and an in-depth training in therapeutic massage.

Applicants should have a minimum of five GCSEs and two passes at A level, and be over the age of 21. The fees are currently (1993–94) £3,000 per annum for each course.

The School is affiliated to the Register of Traditional Chinese Medicine (see p. 25).

The Northern College of Acupuncture

The training programme is on a part-time basis, made up of 44 teaching weekends and 30 clinical training days, structured as follows:

First year. 16 weekends and 10 clinic days, comprising TCM I, acupressure, massage, point location, counselling and Western medicine I (anatomy and physiology).
Second year. 16 weekends and 20 clinic days, comprising TCM II, acupressure, massage, point location, counselling, Western medicine II (pathology).
Third year. 12 weekends, comprising TCM III, Western medicine III (clinical medicine).

Students are expected to do about two hours of study at home for every hour of teaching. A point location exam is set after five terms and must be passed before clinical work can continue. The clinical work is assessed on the ability of the student to diagnose and treat correctly.

The preferred minimum standard for acceptance is five GCSEs and two A levels. The fee for the complete course (payable in five instalments) is currently (1994) £4,490.

The College is affiliated to the Register of Traditional Chinese Medicine (see p. 25).

Registering Organisations

The Council for Acupuncture

The Council for Acupuncture acts as an umbrella organisation for its five recognised professional organisations of acupuncturists. These are: the **British Acupuncture Association and Register** (members being designated MBAcAR); the **Chung San Acupuncture Society** (members being designated MCSAcS); the **International Register of Oriental Medicine** (members being designated MIROM); the **Register of Traditional Chinese Medicine** (members being designated MRTCM); and the **Traditional Acupuncture Society** (members being designated MTAcS). Over 1,100 practitioners are registered with these associations.

Case Study

Zita is both a midwife and acupuncturist who has been practising at a hospital on the NHS since September 1993, providing acupuncture for pregnant and post-natal women alongside normal hospital practice. She works as part of a team in the hospital for 16 hours a week and also works privately from home one day a week. She is a member of both the Royal College of Midwives and the Traditional Acupuncture Society.

Before I knew about acupuncture, I had been working as a community midwife. At that time, I had a child who kept me awake all night. I was sleeping hardly at all and was so, so tired. I went to my GP who offered me sleeping pills which I was unhappy about. It was a neighbour who suggested I should have some acupuncture, which I did, and after six weeks felt very much better. After that, I never looked back! I was able to get a very generous discretionary grant from my local authority to undertake the training at the College of Traditional Acupuncture and trained there for three years. It was a good course which I found fascinating. For me, it all came together at the clinical in the third year.

As an acupuncturist I think it is very important to be able to communicate, to listen and to be there for each individual. And I think it's wonderful that I can combine the skills of both acupuncture and midwifery.

The women who come to me at the hospital are fairly desperate. They are usually referred by their GPs or other midwives because orthodox treatment has not helped their problems. Sometimes they come by word of mouth. In pregnancy, the conditions treated include morning sickness, backache, sciatica, varicose veins, haemorrhoids, carpal tunnel syndrome [pain and numbness in the fingers] and exhaustion. The majority of my patients are antenatal, but there are a few women I treat after they have given birth. Post-natally I treat mastitis [inflammation of the breast], lack of breast milk and pain relief. I always treat not only the problems but the whole person.

The initial consultation for every new patient takes about 45 minutes. I have to find out about the woman's main reason for treatment and also other things such as her temperature, appetite, sleep patterns, bowel movements, circulation and general energy levels. Personal problems in her life at the time may have a bearing on the problem she comes to see me about and are also taken into account. From the information obtained, acupuncture points are chosen and needled. At the next session I ask my patient how she's been and whether she has felt any improvements; different acupuncture points may be used according to the feedback. Every treatment given is individually tailored to the particular woman concerned. Almost all my patients have improved dramatically; the only ones that haven't are those who for one reason or another have been unable to attend for regular treatment sessions.

Acupuncture at the hospital for pre- and post-natal women has now been running for six months and the demands for it are growing each week. We now have two more midwives training to be acupuncturists, so that in the future we hope to be able to provide a full-time service for women, covering labour as well.

I think acupuncture is going through a very exciting time today and right now there is a big move to get it recognised and accepted within the NHS. I'm hoping that lots more nurses and midwives will train in acupuncture, and in other branches of complementary medicine too, so that they can offer a whole range of therapies.

3

The Alexander Technique

Definition and Principles

The Alexander Technique teaches people new ways of thinking and using their bodies with a view to eliminating the effects of unconscious bad habits, such as tension and contorted posture, and thereby improving physical and psychological well-being. A fundamental principle of the Technique is that the mind and body are interconnected and interact with each other.

'Teachers of the Alexander Technique teach. They do not profess to treat, or make extravagant claims to cure' ('The F Matthias Alexander Technique: a short introduction', pamphlet, Patrick Macdonald, 1955). Practitioners of the Technique see it as a way of living rather than a therapy, as a method of promoting well-being through re-education rather than as treating dysfunction. They refer to themselves as teachers and to the people who come to them as pupils, rather than clients or patients. (Students are trainee teachers.) Pupils are taught to become aware of balance, posture and movement applied to all actions in everyday life, such as thinking, breathing, eating, speaking, walking, standing, carrying, reading and writing.

The Technique may be seen to complement conventional medicine.

History

The Alexander Technique is named after its creator, an Australian born in Tasmania, Frederick Matthias Alexander

(1869–1955). He trained as an actor, but began to lose his voice on stage. Medical treatment did not improve his condition, so Alexander investigated the problem himself. After observing himself many times in front of mirrors, he began to realise that his postural habits affected his voice. He deduced that he could cure the problems with his voice by improving his posture, and he noted that the relationship between the head, neck and back was extremely important. His breathing and general well-being also improved.

Alexander came to London in 1904 where he was known as 'The Breathing Man'. Actors and those with respiratory problems came to him for help, and his discoveries became the basis for a technique for retraining the body's movements and positions. In 1931 he started a three-year teacher programme for teachers, based on his findings. He continued to work until his death in 1955.

The Alexander Technique Today

The Alexander Technique today is taught worldwide, predominantly in the UK, the USA, Australia, Israel and in many countries in Europe.

In the UK, demand for Alexander teachers is still growing, conjointly with the growing interest in preventive health care and complementary and alternative medicine. Increasingly, GPs are referring patients to Alexander teachers, approximately 10 per cent of all pupils being referred by GPs and 5 per cent by hospital consultants. Many professional organisations of the creative arts also encourage their members to have lessons in the Technique, including the Guildhall School of Music, the Royal Festival Hall, the Royal College of Music and the Royal Academy of Dramatic Art.

Scientific research is beginning to confirm Alexander's views about the interaction of mind and body and the importance of the postural reflex. Within the last five years there has been growing interest in the Technique shown by the business quarter. Employers are becoming increasingly aware of the need to promote the well-being of their employees to ensure greater productivity. Computing technology has created new problems in the workplace such as repetitive strain injury and a number of back problems. The medical profession has started to recognise that the Alexander Technique can play an effective part in the management of such disorders.

Conditions Used For

Primarily the Technique aims to remove the cause, not the symptoms, of disorders, and teachers do not claim that what they teach is an alternative medicine. It is clear, however, that pupils training in the Technique very often find that there is a reduction and, sometimes, disappearance of some disorders. As breathing, circulation, digestion and elimination processes become easier for the body, as a result of unrestricted movement and improved tone of muscles, so there is greater scope for an individual's own curative powers to take effect. There are many claims that the Technique has not only facilitated an improvement in people's health, but has also contributed towards emotional well-being, mental alertness and resistance to stress. Postural disorders have been alleviated, as well as back pain, breathing problems, repetitive strain injury, hypertension, anxiety, depression, exhaustion, tension headaches, high blood pressure, peptic ulcers, irritable bowel syndrome, colitis, rheumatoid arthritis, osteoarthritis, asthma and a wide range of gynaecological disorders.

It is important to note that teachers of the Alexander Technique are not trained to diagnose diseases; they are not expert in medical problems.

The Technique

Alexander teachers usually work with one pupil only at a time. Initially they watch how pupils use their bodies. Teachers are specially trained to observe and re-educate a person's 'Use' (Alexander's term for the way in which an organism works), defined as the total pattern of coordination in activity as influenced by habit. Their expertise is in re-educating the psycho-physical mechanism. They will have a thorough understanding and experience of change in their own manner of Use, brought about by using the Technique in their daily lives.

Apparently simple activities, such as reading a book, involve the use of many muscles, and there are very many instances of misplaced muscular activity. The modern world is conducive to many stresses and strains, and the emotional and physical demands that we undergo can become fixed in the body in the form of, for instance, chronic muscular tension, which may cause the head, neck and back to be out of alignment. This in turn may cause rounded shoulders, a bowed head, arched back and back pain, with strain on the heart, lungs and digestive system. Teachers use gentle guidance with the hands to help unravel these distortions and at the same time encourage the natural reflexes, the reflexes we are born with, to start working again.

Pupils are taught how to become both psychologically and physically aware of themselves and to learn the basic principles and practice of poise and neuromuscular coordination; they have to learn how to change the habits of a lifetime. They are first taught how to stop an incorrect posture or movement, and are then slowly taken through a simple movement, such as standing up. The teacher will lead pupils through the movement again and again, trying to prevent unaligned movements, until they learn a new way of moving. The teacher will use gentle touch by hand to guide the body into the desired position. At the same time the pupils listen to and act on the teacher's instructions to move, or not move, as directed. By constantly thinking about and practising good posture, they will learn to use their bodies with minimum effort and maximum efficiency. They will learn new, freer ways of moving, sitting, lying down and standing up.

The Alexander Technique does not comprise a set of exercises; it is a way of living daily lives. Therefore it is neither quick nor easy to learn; rather, it is a long-term process involving great commitment and much self-examination. To make a good teacher, the individual might find it helpful to combine an artistic interest in physical self-expression with a scientific interest in anatomy, physiology and psychology. For those who wish to learn the Technique, it is suggested that a course of about 30 lessons of 30–45 minutes each is a good basis, with lessons twice a week for the first 10 to 12 lessons, dropping down to once a week thereafter for a total of about 30 lessons, after which pupils should have learnt enough about the Technique to continue on their own.

The Technique is taught mainly in private practices, teachers' or pupils' homes, adult education centres, health and leisure centres. It is also taught in some hospitals, and voice, back and pain clinics. Some NHS clinics run introductory groups. It is an integral part of courses offered at most major colleges of music and drama.

Training

The following are three-year courses that have been accredited by the Society of Teachers of the Alexander Technique (STAT) (see p. 35) in the UK. All accredited courses must offer at least 1,600 hours of tuition over a period of three years. Unless otherwise stated, the fees for each course are currently (1994) £2,700 per year, necessitating a total outlay of not less than £8,100 for the whole three-year course. The cost of training is high and students are advised to approach their local authorities for a full grant to cover fees and maintenance, bearing in mind that all grants are discretionary. Local authorities that have awarded grants in the past to Alexander students are: Devon County Council, Gloucestershire County Council, Hertfordshire County Council and the London boroughs of Brent, Croydon, Newham, Hackney and Tower Hamlets.

Courses in London

Centre for the Alexander Technique
The curriculum includes the practice of the Technique in its pure form and its application; the recognition of wrong habits of Use; faulty sensory appreciation; and the practice of Inhibition and Direction.

The fees are currently (1994) £3,150 per year, necessitating a total outlay of not less than £9,450.

Centre for Training
There are three 11-week terms per year. Each term consists of three three-week blocks, each separated by a week's break. The curriculum includes a thorough grounding in the principles and practice of the Alexander Technique; an in-depth study of human structure, design and function or misfunction; the emotional and psychological aspects of change and of the teaching situation; and the study of Alexander's books and other writings on the Technique. Students are expected to keep a diary of their

insights and difficulties and to write one or more sizeable papers exploring a subject of their choice relevant to the Technique.

The fees are currently (1994) £4,688 (plus £820 VAT) per year, necessitating a total outlay of not less than £16,524.

The Constructive Teaching Centre Ltd

There are three 13-week terms per year. The curriculum includes the practical study of the principles of the Technique as contained in the writings of Alexander. During the third year students gain experience by teaching in the first-year class. Graduates are encouraged to teach free of charge, with supervision, for a postgraduate term.

The fees are currently (1994) £3,000 (plus £525 VAT) per year, necessitating a total outlay of not less than £10,575.

Hampstead Alexander Centre

There are three terms a year consisting of 13 weeks with two one-week breaks within each term. A structured teaching programme in the first year develops in relation to each individual's needs in the second and third years. The maximum number of students is 10 per class.

The fees are currently (1994) £3,600 per year, necessitating a total outlay of not less than £10,800.

North London Teacher-Training Centre

The curriculum includes a comprehensive study of the Technique, its theory, principles, application and practice; learning to use one's self properly in daily activity and unlearning wrong habits; training in the use of hands and verbal ability to teach the Technique; ongoing study of Alexander's books; and basic anatomy and physiology.

The fees are currently (1994) £3,450 per year, necessitating a total outlay of not less than £10,350.

Victoria Training Course for the Alexander Technique

Potential students are encouraged to attend the school to act as 'bodies' during class before starting their training. There are three 13-week terms per year. The majority of the course consists of practical work in the Technique. This is supplemented by classes in anatomy and physiology and by regular discussion groups. Some written work is also required. Fees: see p. 31.

Courses outside London

Alexander Re-education Centre

There are three 10-week terms per year. The curriculum includes the application of principles laid down in the writings of Alexander, anatomy, physiology, kinesiology and postural reflexes.

The fees are currently (1994) £3,000 per year necessitating a total outlay of not less than £9,000.

Alexander Technique Teaching Centre

There are three 10- or 11-week terms per year. The curriculum includes the development of the student's ability to maintain conscious direction and control in all activities, in particular the use of the hands on pupils; the study of books by Alexander and other relevant authors; the study of anatomy and physiology; and supervised hands-on work with fellow students, teachers and visitors. Fees: see p. 31.

Brighton Alexander Training Centre

There are three terms per year. The curriculum includes the improvement of own self-awareness and body use; the use of hands; the development of manual skills and physical procedures; the practical problems of Alexander teaching; the ongoing study of anatomy; physiology; intellectual and scientific concepts underlying the technique; and consideration of psychological aspects of learning and teaching. There is supervised practice on members of the public in the third year.

The fees are currently (1994) £3,150 (plus £551 VAT), necessitating a total outlay of not less than £11,103.

Bristol Alexander Technique Training School Association

There are three 10- or 12-week terms per year. The curriculum includes understanding the theory and practice of Alexander's principles; recognition of personal responsibility and choice, including the emotional aspects of change and group responsibility; learning hands-on techniques; development of teaching skills; the study of Alexander's books and related literature; lectures on anatomy; physiology and body mapping; use of the voice; discussion groups and talks; and student presentations and written work. Fees: see p. 31.

Essex Alexander School
There are three 10-week terms per year. The curriculum includes 'mini' lessons to improve Use, develop understanding and practice of Inhibition; the development of the powers of observation; the study of the student's psycho-physical Use and 'hands-on' skills; the study of Alexander's books; anatomy and physiology; learning about the importance of language and rapport with pupils; learning to detect negative thinking and its effects; setting up in practice; and presenting the technique to the public. Fees: see p. 31.

North of England Training Centre for the F M Alexander Technique
There are three 12-week terms per year with each term divided into three four-week blocks. The curriculum includes improving the awareness of Use; small groups practising Inhibition and 'non-interference' in a teaching situation; learning to look after one's self while teaching others; applying the Technique to activities – voice work, walking, etc; working in small groups developing hands-on skills; exercises in presenting the Technique in talks, in writing and by demonstration; lectures in basic anatomy, physiology and psychology; and learning about the writings of Alexander and the practice and theory of the Technique, its scientific basis and application in various activities.

The fees are currently (1994) £3,450 per year, necessitating a total outlay of not less than £10,350.

Oxford Alexander Training School
There are three 11-week terms per year. Emphasis is placed on learning to work on one's self and the importance of class sessions. Alexander's books are studied as well as other relevant texts, and some written work is required. There is a weekly anatomy class. Fees: see p. 31.

School of Use
People aged between 20 and 60 may be accepted on to the course. There are three 11- or 13-week terms per year. The School primarily teaches the later views endorsed by Alexander through his own writings. Fees: see p. 31.

West Sussex Centre for the Alexander Technique
There are three 12-week terms per year. The curriculum includes: learning to practice the principles of Inhibition and Direction as formulated by Alexander; the study of his writings and other relevant material; the use of hands on teachers and other students; and, in the third year, working with people from outside the course, including one or two new pupils. Fee: see p. 31.

A graduate from any of the above-mentioned schools is eligible to apply for ordinary (teaching) membership and to have the letters MSTAT after his or her name.

Registering Organisation

Society of Teachers of the Alexander Technique (STAT)
STAT is the umbrella organisation of the Alexander Technique in the UK, formed in 1958 with the aims of maintaining and improving professional standards, making the Technique more widely known, facilitating contact between members, encouraging research and preventing abuse and exploitation by untrained teachers. The Society supervises standards of training, upholds a Code of Ethics and facilitates contact between the public and teachers and contact between members. Regular postgraduate and professional development courses are provided. It has around 550 UK members, designated MSTAT.

Case Study

Hilary, having trained in the Alexander Technique for three years in the 1980s, now teaches the Technique at various centres, as well as privately, in London.

Initially I trained in ballet and, while doing this, strained my back. I heard about the Alexander Technique through some musicians. Later I did a psychology degree at a college and found it a great strain doing the exams. My mother died of a heart attack and I thought I would end up like her if I wasn't careful. There was a lecturer who also taught the Alexander Technique at the college and I initially learnt the Technique from him. It helped me to sort out my old back injury and to cope with high stress levels.

I trained as a teacher at the North London Teacher Training Centre, which I thought was excellent – very warm and caring. Those who taught me had an excellent understanding of the Technique and how to use it. The school's atmosphere was good, which is very important as it enables the students to have the courage to make changes in themselves. There were also a lot of visiting teachers, some of whom gave talks as well as taking part in class activities.

After I finished my training I started to teach the Technique at my home and to run introductory classes in adult education centres in London. I also teach at the Bloomsbury Centre twice a week and run workshops for musicians and various organisations.

I see approximately 20 to 25 people a week. My lessons are either half an hour or 40 minutes each, on a one-to-one basis. I have half the lesson doing simple activities like sitting, standing or walking around while I guide pupils into improving their psycho-physical Use. The other half is devoted to a lying-down procedure on a table. Pupils learn to develop awareness and also learn how to give themselves directions to help themselves. This is important because we can learn to listen to our bodies, to understand how we are within them and how we express ourselves through them. We learn to recognise how, where and why we create patterns of tension and misuse, in response to thoughts, emotions and external stimuli, and how to inhibit and stop habitual patterns of behaviour. Lessons are a process of exploration and discovery. A teacher's hands and verbal instructions guide pupils through activities such as sitting and standing; in that way their misuse may be recognised and a new way of being may be experienced. Once pupils learn to recognise, understand and then inhibit their patterns of misuse, they are freer to choose new and more effective physical and mental responses to situations, while at the same time gaining more awareness, poise and coordination.

I like working with people and find the work very positive and creative. I enjoy helping people to use themselves in a freer manner; it's really rewarding when people's problems or performance levels improve. Also, I find it really positive to have to work on myself at the same time as I work on my pupils.

I would like to see the medical profession become more aware of the Technique through provision of more introductory courses; certainly, outside London there is a shortage of such courses. Perhaps the Technique could be fed into the education system as a preventive measure to stop children's Use deteriorating.

4

Aromatherapy

Definition and Principles

Aromatherapy is an holistic, complementary therapy that can be given together with conventional medicine, used to treat illness and promote good health. A major principle of aromatherapy is that, when used, it supports the body in its fight against disease; it does not, however, necessarily stop the illness.

The therapy involves the systematic use of pure essential oils, obtained from aromatic plants by steam distillation, to improve the balance of the body and mind. These oils are extracted from large quantities of plants, trees and spices. They are usually massaged into the body but may also be inhaled, blended or used in baths.

Although it is not yet understood exactly how aromatherapy works, it is known that essential oils stimulate the sense of smell which in turn affects a region of the brain known as the limbic system, the activity of which is connected with instinctive behaviour, strong emotions and hormone control. Essential oils can temporarily alter our moods and release stress by absorption of small amounts of oils through the skin and into the blood stream, where they have been found to have a physiological effect on the nearby body tissue.

History

Although treatment with essential oils is fairly recent as a healing therapy, its roots can be traced back some 5,000 years. The medicinal use of plant oils is recorded in early Egyptian and Persian empires as well as in early Chinese writings, while the first recorded use of plant oils in Britain was in the thirteenth century.

The first person to use essential oils therapeutically in modern times was a French chemist, Professor René Maurice Gattefossé, working at the beginning of the twentieth century. His interest was aroused when preliminary research showed that essential oils could affect the skin in various ways. Gattefossé recognised their value as antibacterial agents and their potential for treating infections. He realised the importance of research into the chemicals within essential oils and also perceived the psychotherapeutic benefits of scents. His work was later built on by Marguerite Maury, a French biochemist working for the Guerlain scent firm, who investigated the properties of essential oils in the 1940s, and the French physician Dr Jean Valnet, who used essential oils in the 1950s to treat a number of diseases, including cancer, tuberculosis and diabetes.

Aromatherapy Today

In France, aromatherapy is now part of conventional medical treatment. In the UK, however, this is not the case. Along with almost all other complementary and alternative therapies, aromatherapy, although very popular, has not yet received recognition by Parliament. This means, unfortunately, that anyone can set up in practice, sometimes with very little or no training.

Aromatherapy is currently the fastest growing complementary or alternative therapy and doctors and nurses are becoming increasingly aware of its benefits. It is offered in many NHS hospitals, private hospitals and hospices as well as some special schools and prisons. GPs may now employ aromatherapists within their practices and allow them to offer NHS treatments. However, as the 1993 autumn issue of *Nursing Times*, entitled *Complementary Therapy* (Macmillan, p.31), on complementary therapies succinctly states:

> *Lack of approved training and lack of knowledge about raw materials present persistent problems for practitioners who want aromatherapy to be seriously considered. The essential oils are powerful chemicals and practitioners must know exactly what it is they are using; the advice of a trained aromatherapist should always be sought.*

Conditions Used For

Aromatherapy is believed to be very effective in treating nervous problems such as depression, stress and related symptoms such as headaches and insomnia. The therapy has proved successful in treating muscular conditions such as arthritis and cramps, skin problems such as eczema and acne, digestive disorders including colic, diarrhoea and constipation and minor infections such as candidiasis and cystitis. It may also play an important part in the healing of both physical and mental wounds. Aromatherapy is considered to be helpful in the treatment of long-term conditions or recurring illnesses; it can sometimes succeed in treating conditions which are chronic (but not critical), particularly if conventional medicine has proved unsuccessful. Aromatherapy is also very useful for menstrual problems and for the treatment (using low doses of essential oils) of babies and children who refuse medicines.

Essential oils should be used with care as some are toxic in large doses and are irritants to the skin. They should *never* be used undiluted on the skin and should be ingested only when prescribed by a qualified practitioner. A number may cause problems during pregnancy (for example, pennyroyal), and some oils might exacerbate existing health problems.

Aromatherapy treatment is not physically addictive.

Treatment

The initial session between practitioner and patient may last for up to two hours, with a detailed discussion about, and examination of, the patient's health, symptoms, emotions, way of life, diet, exercise taken, posture, appearance and sleeping habits. The therapist will then select the oils considered appropriate for the individual, taking into account both the symptoms and an holistic view of the patient.

Skilled practitioners select from a range of 40 or more different essential oils, according to specific chemical indicators combined with an intuitive understanding of the effect and effectiveness of these oils. Each oil has an affinity for various parts of the body and encourages cellular activity. Combined with the therapeutic effects of massage, essential oils tend to improve the circulation and excrete toxins; they also have a comforting and soothing effect on the whole person. This may be offered as drops on sugar lumps (the oil previously having been diluted in alcohol), in syrups, capsules, compresses, teas, tinctures, lotions, creams or ointments to be used by the patient for home use, or more usually the practitioner gives massage treatment (with the essential oils in a vegetable oil base) which lasts for up to an hour.

Aromatherapists work in private practice, at home or visiting patients in their homes, or in intensive care units in hospitals, in hospices, in geriatric units, with the disabled in day-care centres, in complementary health clinics, or in health clubs and spas.

Training

The Institute of Traditional Herbal Medicine and Aromatherapy

The Institute provides a 200-hour theoretical and practical training, leading to a diploma in aromatherapy massage and bodywork. It comprises 16 weekend sessions held over a period of nine months. No formal qualifications are necessary. The course consists of the following:

Part A: aromatherapy as a healing art. 75 hours of theoretical and practical class study of essential oils and how to use them therapeutically according to the principles of modern science and Traditional Chinese Medicine.

Part B: aromatherapy massage and bodywork. 75 hours of practical training in therapeutic massage, acupressure massage, joint release, soft-tissue bodywork and introductory cranial therapy. These are integrated into a comprehensive system of aromatherapy bodywork.

Part C: anatomy, physiology and basic clinical science. 50 hours of class instruction in scientific anatomy and physiology as well as introductory clinical science (the study of disease).

Part D: practical treatments. 50 full practice treatments involving the submission of 50 treatment reports which incorporate a minimum of 12 case studies.

The fees are currently (1994) £1,595 for the complete course.

Graduates of the diploma course are eligible for membership of the Register of Qualified Aromatherapists (see p. 44). The

Institute is affiliated to the Aromatherapy Organisations Council (see p. 43).

Please note that the Institute teaches aromatherapy only and not medical herbalism.

Shirley Price Aromatherapy Ltd

The School provides an aromatherapy bodywork certificate course of 20 days, comprising four five-day modules. No previous therapeutic training is necessary to gain entry on to the course. GCSEs in English, biology and chemistry are considered advantageous.

Subjects studied include the history of aromatherapy; the philosophy of holistic healing; anatomy and physiology; client relationships; counselling and communication; stress management; contra-indications and cautions; possible toxicity and safety in use; essential oil pathways; skin health; allergy and substance sensitivity; nutrition; massage and bodywork; posture and breathing; relaxation techniques; common ailments; biochemistry pathology; business and practice management; professional association and insurance; and codes and ethics of practice. The course includes exams on anatomy and physiology and the theory and practice of aromatherapy, and 35 case studies have to be completed.

The cost of the course is currently (1994) £1,200 (plus VAT).

The School also provides a clinical practitioners' diploma course which is open to anyone who has obtained the Certificate or the equivalent from a school teaching according to the standards demanded by the Aromatherapy Organisations Council (see p. 43).

The course consists of five days' intensive in-house theory training. The student should submit a dissertation on a chosen aspect of aromatherapy. The following subjects are studied: diagnosis; body analysis; pathology; perplexing oils; clinical dietetics; psychoneuroimmunology; stress management; paediatrics and geriatrics; botany; olfaction and effects; further chemistry; models of disease and health; further *materia medica*; essential oil pathways; counselling and communication; supplementation and prescribing; onward referring and professional cooperation; clinical practice and professionalism; and personal and professional growth and development. After it has been ascertained that the student has completed 200 hours of clinical practice, a clinical diploma in aromatherapy is awarded.

The cost of the course is currently (1994) £315 (plus VAT).

Shirley Price Aromatherapy is registered with the Aromatherapy Organisations Council (see p. 43) and is affiliated to the International Society of Professional Aromatherapists (see p. 44) and the British Complementary Medicine Association (see p. 14).

The School of Holistic Aromatherapy

The School provides a diploma course in aromatherapy, comprising a total of at least 200 hours of class study, which is open to all who want to become professional practitioners (minimum age 21). Students are awarded a diploma in holistic aromatherapy when all parts of the course have been successfully completed. The syllabus is as follows:

Part I: Anatomy and physiology. This comprises 10 sessions covering a period of 40 hours over six months with relevant home study.

Part II: Basic massage. This comprises five or more days tuition on selected weekdays and Saturdays, covering a period of 40 hours with on-going assessment of acquired skills.

Part III: Aromatherapy. This section is concerned with all aspects of aromatherapy necessary to a professional practitioner, including: the place of aromatherapy in the therapeutic world; benefits and limitations of aromatherapy; historical background; botanical origins; properties and characteristics of essential oils; an indepth study of 40 essential oils; methods of extraction, purity and storage; the art of blending; methods of application of aromatherapy; and diagnosis and observation skills. There are 120 hours of tuition and 200 hours or more of assignments and home study.

There is a two-hour written exam on anatomy and physiology and a two-hour practical exam. Students have to complete a file and write up six case studies. A diploma in holistic aromatherapy is awarded when all parts of the course have been successfully completed. Successful completion of the course leads to membership of the International Federation of Aromatherapists (see p. 44).

The cost of the course is currently (1994) as follows: Part I (Anatomy and physiology) £160; Part II (Basic massage) £150; Part III (Aromatherapy) £975.

The School of Holistic Aromatherapy is registered with the International Federation of Aromatherapists (see p. 44) and is affiliated to the Aromatherapy Organisations Council (see below) and the Institute for Complementary Medicine (see p. 15).

The Tisserand Institute

The Institute provides a diploma course in holistic aromatherapy. There are no set prerequisites for entrance on to the course but students are asked to have a commitment to caring, an interest in people, good health and an interest in holistic healing. There are modules in the following subjects: anatomy and physiology; philosophy of healing; chemistry and pharmacology; aromatherapy; clinical medicine; communication skills; massage; kinesiology; nutrition; clinical practice; and practice management.

The course can be taken either full or part time. The length of the full-time course is nine months (52 class days). This includes six months in class with a further three months for completion of case study work. The length of the part-time course is two years (also 52 class days). The content of both courses is the same. Those who receive the diploma are entitled to have the initials TDHA (Tisserand Diploma in Holistic Aromatherapy) after their names.

The cost of both the full- and part-time course is currently (1994) £2,495 (plus VAT), and the venue is the Royal Masonic Hospital in London.

The Tisserand Institute is registered with the Register of Qualified Aromatherapists (see p. 44) and is a member of the Aromatherapy Organisations Council (see below).

Registering Organisations

The Aromatherapy Organisations Council (AOC)

As from 1 January 1994, the minimum supervised in-class education and training required to become an AOC recognised aromatherapist is as follows: anatomy and physiology, 40 hours; massage (whole body), 60 hours; aromatherapy 80 hours. The training period from start to qualification (including practice to complete case studies) must be at least nine months.

The International Federation of Aromatherapists (IFA)

The Federation is involved with many educational programmes and was instrumental in introducing aromatherapy into the NHS, private hospitals, hospices, special schools and prisons. It has instigated a number of research programmes into the physiological and psychological effects of aromatherapy and is the largest established organisation for professional aromatherapists in the world. The UK alone has over 1,000 members.

The Federation has established a system of registration for training establishments with an external examination for people who apply for full membership. Only candidates who have attended a course approved by the Federation and have completed at least 200 hours of practical and theoretical clinical training are eligible to take the exams that must be passed in order to become a full member of the IFA. In addition to aromatherapy, the exams test knowledge of basic massage, anatomy and physiology. Full members are entitled to use the initials MIFA after their names.

The International Society of Professional Aromatherapists (ISPA)

The primary aim of ISPA is to develop and stimulate high professional standards. The approved aromatherapy course should be of the following minimum duration: aromatherapy/essential oils (minimum 20 oils) 50 hours; anatomy and physiology 40 hours; massage 60 hours. The total hours should be spread over a minimum period of nine months. In addition, case histories should be based on 10 clients, each receiving treatment on several occasions and for at least 60 hours in total. ISPA arranges postgraduate training on a regular basis. Full members are entitled to use the initials MISPA after their names.

The Register of Qualified Aromatherapists

The aims of the Register are to establish, encourage and foster high standards of training and practice in the field of aromatherapy massage, to act as a forum for the exchange of knowledge, expertise and research information relevant to the practice of professional aromatherapy, and to promote a fuller understanding among the general public of the benefits of aromatherapy massage and bodywork as well as the requirements for its ethical and professional practice. The Register has over 100 members. Members are entitled to have the initials MRQA after their names, signifying membership.

Case Study

Nicole has worked as an aromatherapist for many years and seven years ago set up her own training school. She lives in London.

I have found London the most wonderful place for complementary medicine; it is the centre in Europe. Everything is in one place, and people can practise freely as the law is only concerned with malpractice. It amuses me that in London everyone appears to be busy with some form of healing. It is a great centre for spiritual growth.

I came to aromatherapy long ago, through being involved with astrology and psychic healing. It came to the point where I felt I needed to do something physical with people. I had been using other body therapies and essential oils for meditation purposes, so I knew about the basics. Then I went on holiday to France and talked at length to my uncle who is a homoeopath doctor and uses essential oils in complicated cases. I began to discover aromatherapy in depth and from then on I kept on learning.

I have roughly 10 clients a week. I used to have a lot more but found it was too much. The number I have now is just right. When I give aromatherapy treatment to a client, I first make sure he or she is comfortable. I describe the treatment and take a detailed medical history at the first session. Once I've decided what to use, I'll mix a blend. I often use a small, heated pad to keep the client warm. Massage can make people feel cold, you know; it lowers blood pressure. I begin with a gentle touch and work rhythmically to release body tension in such a way that the client lets go of the body bit by bit. Clients always hold very strong tensions in the neck. The overall effect of the combination of the smells of the essential oils and the massage is semi-hypnotic.

Whatever state clients arrive in for a session, aromatherapy will break down their barriers; it opens them up without intruding into their private lives. Clients feel they have more space in their bodies; they become quite laid back and often look a lot younger when the session is finished. They lose their masks. I just love that.

People get to know themselves better, both emotionally and physically. They begin to manage themselves better. If someone chooses to change then this will happen, but more often I see the flourishing of a person's true potential rather than a true change. In order to change, people have to apply aromatherapy to their lives, to make the therapy a way of life.

It's wonderful that aromatherapy has generated such an interest. We who work in the field should, I think, make every effort to build bridges so that we can connect with each other and work together to create higher standards. But the therapy must not become academic or rigid. Whatever happens, it must retain its individual, intuitive character.

5

Chiropractic

Definition and Principles

Chiropractic is formed from the Greek words *cheiro* (hand) and *praktikos* (to use) and means 'done by hand'. Chiropractors diagnose by feeling (palpation) and treat disorders of the spine, joints and muscles by manual manipulation, sometimes with the help of X-rays. They prefer the word 'adjustment' rather than manipulation because they claim this word signifies more control, specificity and skill. Drugs and surgery are never used. It is a complementary rather than an alternative discipline to conventional medicine.

History

The art of spinal manipulation goes back at least 2,000 years. Greek and Egyptian manuscripts refer to the practice, while ancient Chinese, Hindus and Babylonians are known to have used manipulation to treat a range of health problems. The founder of the present-day practice of chiropractic was a Canadian called Daniel David Palmer. He based his ideas on the beliefs of Hippocrates who claimed we should look at the spine for the basic cause of disease. Knowing that the spine protects the spinal cord and nerves emanating from the spine, Palmer believed that if any section of the spine were to be disturbed, however slightly, this would cause an interference with some of the nerve impulses which travel through the spinal cord. He concluded that if the parts of the spine which had been disturbed were to be readjusted, this would once more allow the nerve impulses to travel freely.

Modern-day chiropractic first appeared in the USA at the end of the last century and in Europe a little before the First World War.

Chiropractic Today

When chiropractic was newly established at the beginning of this century there was great opposition from the ranks of orthodox medicine. In the United States many practitioners were imprisoned, with Bartlett J Palmer, the son of Daniel David Palmer, being described as 'the most dangerous man in Iowa out of a prison cell'. The practice now, however, has achieved worldwide respectability and there have been no fewer than six formal government enquiries into chiropractic during the past 25 years. Today, chiropractic is the world's largest healing profession after medicine and dentistry, and over 50 per cent of the profession has qualified since 1980. Legislation licensing the practice of chiropractic exists in 17 countries throughout the world, including the USA, Canada, Australia, New Zealand, Mexico and Switzerland.

At present in the UK there is no legislation for chiropractic, but equally there is no law forbidding it. The British Chiropractic Association (see p. 54) applied to join the NHS in 1974. Although it was rejected, the General Medical Council ruled in 1977 that doctors could refer their patients to a chiropractor provided they retained clinical responsibility. A 1986 survey of GPs showed that 50 per cent had referred patients to chiropractors and osteopaths for non-medical spinal manipulation over the preceding 12 months.

A random controlled trial under the auspices of the British Medical Research Council, involving 741 people and published in the *British Medical Journal* in June 1990, showed that patients with either acute or chronic lower back pain of mechanical origin obtained excellent results under chiropractic care and that benefit remained for a long time after treatment had finished. Chiropractic was compared with hospital outpatient treatment and physiotherapy. The conclusion was that chiropractic treatment was significantly more effective. The report concluded that: 'consideration should be given to providing chiropractic within the NHS'.

The number of people within the profession is likely to double within the next five years. Currently (1994) there are around 800 qualified and registered chiropractors in the UK treating 75,000 patients a week. Most registered chiropractors cooperate fully with hospital doctors and GPs.

At present there are no effective sanctions against unlicensed, untrained or professionally negligent practitioners, but there are moves to ensure that unqualified people cannot use the title. The three bodies governing the chiropractic profession in the UK – the British Chiropractic Association, the Institute of Pure Chiropractic and the British Association for Applied Chiropractic – have decided to set up a single Council and Register of Chiropractors, which is based on an Act of Parliament, incorporating all chiropractors practising in the UK. The Council will be responsible for the educational standards and professional conduct of the profession. An Act to register the chiropractic profession was passed in Parliament in July 1994.

Conditions Used For

Four out of five people are known to have back problems at some time during their lives – in the UK nearly 90,000 people every day are unable to work as a result of back pain. Chiropractic is used to treat conditions such as lumbago (lower back pain), slipped disc, or sciatica (pain running down the back and outside of the thigh, leg and foot). It is also used to treat a wide range of other common aches and pains, including headaches, and in particular migraine, and hip and knee problems, as well as sporting injuries, hay fever, catarrh and vertigo. Chiropractic has also proved beneficial for period pains, rheumatism, dizziness, tinnitus, pins and needles, asthma, indigestion, constipation and numbness. Treatment is not given, however, if there is inflammation, any other signs of infection, or tumours in the spine.

Treatment

The profession's main focus has always been on the relationship between the impaired movement of spinal vertebrae and the central nervous system, and the effect this has on health. The spinal column comprises 24 movable vertebrae, sacrum and coccyx. Vertebral misalignments known as subluxations can occur which can interfere with and impinge on the nerves emanating between the vertebrae, causing subsequent nerve dysfunction. There are very many types of manipulation or adjustment that can be applied to joints, muscles and bodily tissues. The art of chiropractic is knowing how, when and where to perform these adjustments so that normal, healthy mechanical function of the spine is restored. The practitioner treats a 'fixation' which is the restriction of movement in a joint affecting other structures and tissues. The chiropractor adjusts the spine to restore a full range of movement and relaxes the muscles, thereby reducing inflammation and pain. Chiropractors spend years learning about the intricacies of human (and sometimes animal) anatomy so that with the use of their eyes and hands, and sometimes with the help of X-rays, they can effect the necessary adjustment. A chiropractor has to find out not only what has gone wrong but why, so that bad habits are corrected and a recurrence of the problem becomes less likely. There will be a focus on the patient's daily life and habits and the need for him or her to take on responsibility for health care.

Once they have trained, junior practitioners become attached to established practitioners and may well work in several locations before they become established themselves.

Training

There are three chiropractic schools in the UK which train practitioners using their own particular techniques. Each provides education and training, details of which are set out below.

The Anglo-European College of Chiropractic
The Anglo-European College of Chiropractic is the only chiropractic college in Europe to offer a four-year full-time degree course which is a BSc (Hons) in Human Science (Chiropractic), together with a full-time fifth year postgraduate diploma (Chiropractic) (designated DC). The degree course was the first degree course in complementary medicine to be recognised in the UK. In 1991–92 a total of 374 students were studying it.

Students must be aged 18 or over and have at least two A levels in natural sciences or (in Scotland) four passes in SCE highers with a minimum B pass to include two natural science subjects. Mature students are accepted provided they have either A level chemistry, A level human biology or A level biology; or the Open University Science Foundation Course (S102); or a suitable science-based Access course. Completed application forms together with an admission fee of £15 have to reach the College Registry between 1 September and 31 March prior to the year of entry. In addition, adequate financial provision to cover the entire course is required.

The syllabus comprises the following:

Year 1: human physics, human chemistry, human anatomy (I), human physiology (I), histology, microbiology, introduction to palpation and biomechanics, basic radiology, chiropractic contextual studies (I), health studies, essential computing, interpersonal skills and study skills.

Year 2: human anatomy (II), human physiology (II), clinical biomechanics, basic radiology, chiropractic contextual studies (II), introduction to diagnosis, nutrition and psychology.

Year 3: pathological anatomy, pathology, orthopaedics and extra spinal, chiropractic technique (I), neurology, diagnostic radiology (I), general diagnosis (I) and research methodology.

Year 4: chiropractic technique (II), clinical radiography, applied neurology, diagnostic radiology (II), chiropractic diagnosis and therapy (I), clinic preparation/patient communication, research project and clinic management.

Year 5: chiropractic diagnosis and therapy (II), auxiliary therapy, clinical pharmacology, obstetrics/gynaecology, clinical sociology, dermatology, geriatrics, paediatrics, guest lectures, general diagnosis (II) and clinical internship.

The programme leads to the award of the BSc (Hons) at the end of the fourth year and the postgraduate diploma on completion of the fifth year. Graduates are then required to complete a minimum of one year's supervised clinical practice. Students who do not complete the programme may be awarded the DipHE Human Sciences if they have successfully completed the first two years of the programme. The various elements of the programme are continuously assessed by a combination of assignments, examinations and assessment of clinical competence.

The College clinic handles an average of 30,000 outpatient visits per year. Students, having passed their Clinic Entrance exams, work with these patients under close supervision.

The research department has an ongoing programme of post-graduate investigations into the fields of biomechanics, neuro-physiology and field research.

The fees for one year are currently (1994) set at over £5,500.

The McTimoney Chiropractic School

The School, which was founded in 1972, was named after John McTimoney who refined and developed the original Daniel David Palmer chiropractic training into a total chiropractic method that reintegrated the whole body structurally. His approach was based on the belief that the main cause of disease and pain was misalignment of bone causing interference with the nerve supply. He used only touch and observation to detect and correct misalignments.

The aim of a McTimoney chiropractic treatment is to remove any interference with the body's nerve supply. McTimoney chiropractors treat a patient holistically and use no instruments other than the hands of the practitioner, no medication and no X-rays. They are taught a special technique which utilises a high velocity, low amplitude thrust, known as toggle recoil. Students are trained to know when to use the technique and when not to use it, to manage a medical practice efficiently, to learn basic patient–practitioner skills and to be able to communicate effectively with fellow healthcare professionals.

The McTimoney Chiropractic School specialises in developing in its students an acutely sensitive touch and teaches a gentle but thorough whole-body treatment. The training lasts four years part time. The curriculum includes physics, chemistry, anatomy, physiology, biomechanics, basic radiology, myology and differential diagnosis. Intensive clinical teaching is given, with individual tutorial supervision by experienced practising chiropractors. The School operates a continuous assessment system, through a combination of assignments, exams and tests of clinical competence, culminating in a final exam validated by external examiners.

The School is realigning its courses to the standard academic year so that all new courses will in future start in the autumn. The course is currently part time, allowing students to continue in employment elsewhere. Negotiations are in hand to validate the present course nationally at diploma level and this will later be extended to degree level to agree with European standards for chiropractic education.

Candidates for the course must be over 18 and have passes in five GCSE subjects, including English, maths, chemistry and biology or a double combined science, and have two passes at A level, including natural sciences. Mature students are accepted, provided they have either A level chemistry, human biology, biology, the Open University Science Foundation Course (S 102) or other suitable science-based Access courses. Completed application forms, together with a fee of £20, must reach the Registrar by 30 April.

The McTimoney chiropractic course for animals is an 18-month postgraduate part-time course open only to qualified McTimoney practitioners. It involves home study and attendance at regular theoretical and practical tutorials. In addition to animal anatomy and physiology, a wide range of related equine, canine and vertebrate animal subjects are covered.

Fees are currently (1994) £1,855 for a year's training.

The Witney School of Chiropractic
The School was set up by Hugh Corley who was taught by John McTimoney. Corley evolved the McTimoney–Corley Method of practising chiropractic which incorporates McTimoney's whole-body approach together with a special reflex recoil adjustment technique that forms the basis of this method of treatment. Students who learn and subsequently teach at the Witney School are known as McTimoney–Corley chiropractors.

The course of study, based on a modular learning system, lasts four years. The minimum age of entry is 18. An A level standard of education is desirable but not essential, and an entrance exam may be required. The courses are designed to enable people to study chiropractic while continuing in their existing employment. The first three years consists of both theoretical and practical work running in parallel. Exams are taken on a progressive basis throughout the course of study. The fourth year involves clinical experience and expansion of techniques under the guidance of established practitioners. There is also a probationary fifth year where newly qualified students will be required to practise under supervision. At the end of the fourth year, subject to having submitted an acceptable thesis, the student will be awarded a School Diploma in Chiropractic.

The subjects studied are medical physics, biomechanics, clinical diagnosis, radiology, business technology, public speaking and applied counselling.

The Witney School of Chiropractic also provides an 18-month course in Animal Chiropractic for those who have already qualified in the above course.

Students have to pay their own fees. Currently (1994) these are £1,860 per year. Grants may be available from the local education authority but they are not available from the school.

Registering Organisations

The British Association for Applied Chiropractic
This is the professional regulatory body of McTimoney–Corley chiropractors. At present (1994) it has about 60 practitioner members, designated BAAC.

The British Chiropractic Association
This was set up in 1925 as the governing and registering body of the Anglo-European College of Chiropractic. At present (1994) it has about 525 practitioner members, designated BCA.

The Institute of Pure Chiropractic
This is the associated registration and disciplinary body for graduates from the McTimoney Chiropractic School. At present (1994) it has about 200 practitioner members. MC designates a qualified McTimoney chiropractor, while MIPC indicates membership of the Institute.

6

Herbal Medicine

Definition and Principles

Herbal medicine can be defined as the art and science of using plant remedies both for healing and for ensuring continuing good health. Some, but not all, herbal practitioners describe themselves as phytotherapists, derived from the Greek *phyton*, 'plant', and *therapeuein*, meaning 'to take care of' or 'heal'.

Herbal medicine is essentially holistic, in that each person is treated as a whole and unique individual. It is the traditional European medicine, pre-dating allopathic medicine by thousands of years.

History

Herbal medicine is the oldest system of medicine in the world and every country has used plants for medicinal purposes.

In China herbs have played a very important part in the country's history, especially in health care. As long ago as 2500 BC a Chinese herbal listed 365 remedies, while papyri from Egypt, dated 1550 BC, described 700 plant medicines. Much of Europe's knowledge of herbs may be traced to the Greeks and Egyptians, whose priests were also herbal practitioners, and the philosophy behind Western herbalism has been strongly influenced by Ayuvedic medicine, the traditional system of medicine in India, dealing with every aspect of mental, physical and spiritual health.

During the Middle Ages in Britain, nunneries and monasteries had physic gardens in which medicinal plants were grown. People living locally were treated for their illnesses in pharmacies and hospitals with remedies obtained from these plants. With the growth of allopathic medicine in the seventeenth century, however, practitioners of herbal medicine gradually fell out of favour. In 1864 a number of herbalists founded the National Association (later Institute) of Medical Herbalists (see p. 62) which resisted, and still resists today, attempts by orthodox medical pressure groups to have the alternative medicine banned. Herbal therapy nevertheless remained popular with the general public, especially in Scotland, the north of England, Ireland and Wales, and there were herbalists in most towns until the end of the Second World War. The discipline probably reached an all-time low with the advent of the NHS in 1948 which originally provided allopathic medicines free of charge.

Herbal Medicine Today

Worldwide, the medicinal use of plants is the major form of medicine today and is encouraged by the World Health Organization. International scientific research has confirmed many ancient beliefs about the medicinal properties of plants. It has also widened herbalists' knowledge. Even so, it has been estimated that there are over three-quarters of a million species of plants which have yet to be examined for possible therapeutic use.

In the UK today, herbal medicine is becoming increasingly popular and widespread, and an ever-growing number of professional herbalists treat patients for very many illnesses. Chinese herbal medicine in particular has seen spectacular expansion over the last five years; there are now (1994) around 600 Chinese herbal clinics. However, it should be noted that the stringent requirements laid on the pharmaceutical chemical industry to prove the efficacy and safety of their products bear hard on herbal medicine. The 1968 Medicines Act defined a herbal remedy as:

A medicinal product consisting of a substance produced by subjecting a plant or plants to drying, crushing or any other process, or of a mixture whose sole ingredients are two or more substances so produced, or of a mixture whose sole ingredients are one or more substances so produced and water or some other inert substance.

Herbal practitioners may thus dispense and supply dried herbs, mixtures prepared from herbal tinctures or extracts, purely herbal ointments, employing an inert base only. A medical herbalist may prescribe 'in accordance with his own judgement as to the treatment required'.

At present, no licence is required to sell any plant or mixture of plants which are dried, cut or powdered, provided the label bears only the name and state of the plants. (A licence is, however, required for over-the-counter remedies.) There has recently been pressure from the Royal Pharmaceutical Society to license herbs on account of the very small number of deaths attributed to toxic herbs being prescribed, but this would almost certainly prove financially prohibitive due to the cost of testing each plant ingredient. It would seem necessary, though, to ensure a high standard of training, skills and practice by setting up an accrediting organisation which would license practitioners who have reached acceptable standards.

Conditions Used For
There are records of herbal treatment for practically all known human diseases. Herbal remedies are particularly beneficial for skin disorders, insomnia, digestive problems, migraines, rheumatism, arthritis, menstrual disorders, respiratory infections, allergies, heart and circulatory problems, stress-related conditions and depression. Biochemical changes to ensure good health can be effected by various plant extracts; for example, to maintain a fluid balance and to stimulate the body's defence mechanisms.

There are a number of herbs which the Department of Health states carry a potential health risk. Pennyroyal and broom can cause miscarriage, bearberry and ragwort have been linked with liver damage, and mistletoe with gastroenteritis, while feverfew, if taken raw, may cause mouth ulcers (in tablet form, however, it is not harmful). In 1993, comfrey tablets and capsules were banned in the UK, owing to the perceived high levels of pyrrolizidine alkaloids, believed to cause liver damage in experiments with laboratory rats. Comfrey tisanes and creams, however, are still permitted.

Herbal remedies are not physically addictive.

Treatment

The purpose of medical herbal treatment is to assist the recuperative processes in the body to re-establish the physiological balance of health. At the first consultation, the practitioner will take a detailed case history to establish the cause of ill health and also any underlying imbalances. A physical examination will help with the diagnosis. Western medical herbalists are likely to take a patient's blood pressure, use X-rays and take samples of blood and urine for analysis; their diagnostic tools and techniques are similar to those of GPs. Chinese medical herbalists, however, adopt the principles and techniques of Traditional Chinese Medicine (TCM) which has radically different methods of diagnosis and treatment (see p. 17). The Western practitioner will suggest possible lifestyle changes, such as dietary changes, exercise, rest and how to cope with stress. An appropriate prescription will then be dispensed for the patient. At the second and subsequent consultations, the patient's condition will be reviewed and changes in remedies prescribed will be made as necessary.

Herbal medicine draws on the whole of the plant world for its sources, including shrubs, trees and seaweed. The various organs, such as the rhizome, stem, roots, berries, leaves, bark, flowers or seeds, or the entire plant, may be used. Medical herbalists disagree with the allopathic approach of isolating and synthesising an active principle, such as aspirin from willow bark, claiming that the active ingredients taken out of context in the long term are incompatible with good health. Instead they advocate that plant materials are a naturally balanced combination of chemicals which offset each other's action and reduce the incidence of damaging side effects.

Remedies may be made from plants anywhere in the world. They are harvested, then stored and processed. Plant medicines are usually prescribed in liquid form as tinctures, fluid extracts or syrups, but may occasionally be given dried to be taken as infusions or decoctions, or in powdered form as tablets or capsules. Ointments, lotions and poultices may also be prescribed as required.

In addition to assessing the patient's sympton. tioner will evaluate the overall balance of the body's s, discover underlying disharmonies. Different remedies ma, given to treat two people apparently suffering from the same complaint. It is the whole person who is being treated, not the disease. Every person responds differently to treatment so it is not possible to say how many consultations will be required.

Training

National Institute of Medical Herbalists

The Institute is currently (June 1994) planning a BSc course in herbal medicine (phytotherapy) at Middlesex University which has been validated and which will start in October 1994. The course will take three or four years (depending on whether it is for academic or professional purposes) full time, or up to six years part time, and it will attract a mandatory grant. The course will remain true to the basic tenets of herbal medicine, with the use and study of the whole plant rather than isolates, treatment of the whole person rather than the disease, and rejection of animal experimentation for research.

The course will cover the full range of medical sciences, anatomy, physiology, pathology, diagnostic skills and clinical examination; it will also cover the full range of herbal medicine, pharmacognosy, *materia medica*, pharmacology (herbal and orthodox), herbal therapeutics and medical ethics. It will cover certain allied skills in depth, such as communication skills, pharmacy, massage and nutritional medicine, and will also carry aromatic medicine and Chinese herbal medicine as options.

The School of Phytotherapy (Herbal Medicine)

The School offers a four-year course, comprising three years of theoretical and practical tuition, followed in the fourth year by a series of specialist seminars and clinical training. The course provides a comprehensive training in herbal medicine and includes an analysis of the principles and philosophy of medical herbalism, an investigation of the constituents and pharmacology of medicinal plants, a study of the human body in health and disease, as well as practical training in relevant diagnostic and therapeutic techniques. In addition to the tuition given, it is necessary for students to undertake several hours of self-study and also to complete 500 hours of clinical training. Final written exams are held at the end of the third year and the final clinical exam at the end of the fourth year. Successful candidates are awarded a diploma and may use the letters DipPhyt (Diploma in Phytotherapy) after their names.

Entrance requirements are two A levels, at least one of which should be science based, and GCSE or O level English language. The fees are currently (1994) £3,600 per year, necessitating a total outlay of not less than £14,400.

There is also a four-year tutorial course, comprising home study, practical seminars and 500 hours of clinical training. Home study averages 20–30 hours per week and written exams take place on completion of second and fourth year studies. A final clinical exam will be held after the fourth year written papers.

Entrance requirements are two A levels, at least one of which should be science based, and GCSE or O level English language. The fees are currently (1994) £475, necessitating a total outlay of not less than £1,900.

There is also a course designed for professionals, such as GPs or osteopaths, who already have substantial clinical experience. The course comprises home study on a tutorial basis, practical seminars and clinical training, and is designed to take approximately 1–2 years to complete. Successful candidates are awarded a certificate.

The fees are currently (1994) £180 per quarter.

The governing body and registering organisation of the School is the National Institute of Medical Herbalists (see p. 62).

The School of Chinese Herbal Medicine
The School provides a two-year diploma course in Chinese herbal medicine, run under the auspices of the Nanjing College of Traditional Chinese Medicine. The syllabus is as follows:

Part 1: Materia medica. A detailed study of about 200 herbs.
Part 2: Prescriptions. About 100 prescriptions are studied in detail which include name, history, ingredients, preparation, functions and uses.

Part 3: Internal medicine. The differentiation and herbal treatment of about 50 common conditions.

Part 4: Clinical practice. Students must complete at least 100 hours of clinical practice before receiving their diploma. Three-quarters of this clinical practice (75 hours) is provided during the course. The remaining 25 hours must either be completed at approved training clinics provided by the School or at the Nanjing College of TCM.

Part 5: Pharmacy and posology. Discussions and practical demonstrations of the preparation of herbs, dosage, storage dispensing and the making of tinctures and ointments.

There are two exams, one at the end of each year.

The course is open to second- and third-year students and graduates of acupuncture colleges, bona-fide practitioners of acupuncture and third- or fourth-year students or practitioners of Western herbalism.

The fees are £1,100 per year or £2,200 for the complete course.

The school is affiliated to the Register of Chinese Herbal Medicine (see p. 62).

Registering Organisations

The British Herbal Medicine Association (BHMA)

The BHMA was founded to advance the science and practice of herbal medicine in the UK and to ensure its continued statutory recognition at a time when all medicines were becoming subject to great regulatory control. It has supported the interests of its members by giving advice and comment on legislation and by providing scientific information. The objectives of the BHMA are to defend the right of the public to choose herbal remedies and to be able to obtain them freely; to encourage wider knowledge and recognition of the value of herbal medicine; to advance the science and practice of herbal medicine by modern techniques; to promote high standards of quality and safety in herbal remedies; and to foster research into phytotherapy.

The BHMA Scientific Committee has developed monographs of plant drugs and provides technical information to BHMA members and public bodies. It was instrumental in publishing the *British Herbal Pharmacopoeia* in 1983, with specifications and therapeutic information.

In 1989 the BHMA became a founder member of the European Scientific Cooperative for Phytotherapy (ESCOP), together with comparable organisations from Belgium, France, Germany, the Netherlands and Switzerland. The aims of ESCOP are to advance the status of herbal medicines throughout Europe and to assist with harmonisation of their regulatory status at the European level.

The General Council and Register of Consultant Herbalists
The Council was incorporated to set up a register of trained medical herbalists, qualified by examination. Facilities are available for members to take out an indemnity insurance against claims made by patients for negligence. There are about 200 members (designated MRH).

The National Institute of Medical Herbalists
The Institute was established in 1864. Its approximately 350 members are graduates of the School of Phytotherapy. Membership, designated by the letters MNIMH, is by examination after completing a four-year course of training. Members have to adhere to a strict Code of Ethics and Practice and are professionally insured.

The Register of Chinese Herbal Medicine
The Register is a professional body created to safeguard and promote the interests of practitioners of Traditional Chinese Medicine (TCM) and the welfare of their patients. Its approximately 120 members, designated by the letters MRCHM, have passed recognised courses in Chinese herbal medicine and have fulfilled the requisite standards required by the Register. Services provided for members include full professional indemnity insurance and a Code of Practice and Ethics.

Case Study

Elisabeth has practised for many years as a medical herbalist in London. She undertook a four-year training course.

I have always loved plants; this comes both from my grand-

mother and mother. My grandfather had a huge garden and I had the run of it – I was there as much as I could be. In the early 1970s in Amsterdam I was given a book on herbal medicine. Later I found the National Institute of Medical Herbalists and my studies took off from there. I did a four-year correspondence course. It was a very thorough training in medical science, covering anatomy, physiology, pathology, pharmacology, differential diagnosis, materia medica (learning about the constituents of plants and how they work), obstetrics, gynaecology, paediatrics and psychiatry. I loved pharmacology best of all, understanding the actions, the active principles of plants – I got a prize for my work! We did clinical training supervised by qualified practitioners for the last two years of our training.

After I finished the course I ran a training clinic for herbal students, first in Tunbridge Wells and then in London. Later I joined an all-women collective of complementary practitioners. I taught and lectured in the Inner London Education Authority and Workers' Educational Association classes all over London and came across people who subsequently came to us for treatment – we were not allowed to advertise as practitioners in herbal medicine. We also liaised with local GPs.

After about three years I left the collective and set up in private practice on my own in my home in Hackney in East London. I would see patients on average about six times at two-weekly intervals. I gave them medicine made from herbs I had picked myself. Each prescription was unique to each patient. At each visit I might change the prescription. I also prescribed vitamin and mineral supplements and usually suggested patients should alter their diet in some respects. Counselling is always part of the job. If appropriate, I would undertake physical examinations of heart, blood pressure, lungs, etc. As I worked mainly with women I did smear tests and internal examinations. I worked a lot with infertile women and had good results. I made my own medicines, tinctures, creams and lotions. This was important as I needed to have an intimate relationship with my tools for healing.

I would very much like to see herbal medicine becoming part of the NHS. For example, herbalists could work in GPs' surgeries on a sessional basis. Apart from being beneficial to patients this would be extremely cost-effective. And it would be a professional service – the training provided by the medical herbal organisations is extremely comprehensive and of a very high quality.

Practitioners of herbal medicine are rare within complementary and alternative medicine; they understand medical jargon and can talk to GPs.

There are problems within the pharmaceutical industry so far as herbal remedies are concerned, with lots of bogus scares, and there is a lot of ignorance on the part of both the medical profession and general public as to what the profession is all about. Nevertheless, I do think herbalism is becoming more popular. I feel very strongly that it is the medicine of the people. It's simple and safe.

7

Homoeopathy

Definition and Principles

Homoeopathy provides a complementary service but has an alternative philosophy of health and disease. The word 'homoeopathy' is derived from the Greek *homoios*, meaning like and *pathos*, meaning suffering. There are several major principles which are unique to this therapy. The first is the Law of Similars – 'that which makes sick shall heal'. A substance which produces the symptoms of a disease may also cure it, expressed in the Latin *similia similibus curentur* (like cures like). When a person has homoeopathic treatment, a substance is used which, in a healthy person, produces symptoms and signs similar to those presented by the patient.

The second principle is the notion of the minimum dose. Plant, mineral and animal substances, as well as products of disease, are used to make homoeopathic remedies. The substance is first soaked in alcohol to extract the active ingredients. The resulting mixture, called the mother tincture, is progressively diluted many times over in measures of tens or hundreds with a vigorous shaking, known as succussion, either by hand or in a purpose-built machine, after each dilution. The shaking is said to 'potentise' the mixture and increase its therapeutic powers. Lower potencies have been subjected to less dilution and succussion than higher potencies and are not usually as powerful and long lasting in their effects.

A third principle is the notion of the uniqueness of the remedy. A remedy is specific to a particular patient at a particular time and stimulates the body's immune system to be strengthened against all illness, not just a single disease. The duration of action of a remedy varies, from hours in acute illnesses, when frequent repetition of remedies is called for, to months, years or even a lifetime. It is important not to take further doses or any other remedy as long as the remedy is still acting. In acute cases the remedy may change rapidly but in chronic cases it may remain the same for months or even years, known as constitutional prescribing.

It is not thought that an individual is sick because of certain symptoms; rather, that symptoms are an individual's expression of 'dis-ease' and that the 'vital force', that is, the body's own curative power, is out of balance and not functioning properly.

Allopathic drugs are occasionally prescribed if the condition requires them – for example, a diabetic must have insulin. It has been found that the therapy often prevents the need for invasive surgery.

History

Samuel Hahnemann, a German doctor, living 200 years ago, did not believe in the orthodox medical practices of the time, such as leeching or purging. He tested 90 substances on healthy volunteers, including himself, his family and friends, and catalogued their effects. Many of the substances were diluted poisons and Hahnemann claimed the more diluted the substance the more effective it became. He therefore suggested that small rather than large doses of his remedies would be safer as they would produce fewer side effects while still remaining effective. Nowadays approximately 2,000 substances have been tested and the list is growing. According to Hahnemann's ideas, in his book the *Organon*, first published in 1810, the first and only duty of the homoeopath is to effect healing by the safest, most gentle, quickest, most reliable and most permanent means known.

The British Homoeopathic Society (now the Faculty of Homoeopathy) was set up in 1844 and faced very great opposition from the orthodox medical establishment of the time. The London Homoeopathic Hospital opened in 1850 and in 1854, during the cholera epidemic, recorded mortality figures of only 16.4 per cent, compared with an average of 61.8 per cent for all other London hospitals.

When the NHS came into being in 1948, existing homoeopathic hospitals were incorporated, operating as special health authorities.

Homoeopathy Today

Homoeopathy is a widely accepted alternative therapy in France, Germany and India. In the UK homoeopathy is classed as being outside mainstream treatment, this despite the fact that it is recognised by Act of Parliament and that there are five homoeopathic hospitals operating within the NHS. These are The Royal London Homoeopathic Hospital, The Glasgow Homoeopathic Hospital, Mossley Hill Hospital, in Liverpool, the Bristol Homoeopathic Hospital and Tunbridge Wells Homoeopathic Hospital. Each is staffed by doctors who are fully qualified through conventional medical training. They have all taken a postgraduate homoeopathic training course, sometimes at the hospital concerned, followed by a written exam or thesis, to become a Member or Fellow of the Faculty of Homoeopathy (see p. 72).

At present, although anyone can set up as a homoeopath, standards have been set by the Society of Homoeopaths (see p. 72). It is possible that a system of state registration for homoeopaths will be created in the near future. GPs are free to provide treatment in accordance with homoeopathic principles.

Conditions Used For

Homoeopathic remedies may be used for almost any reversible illness in adults and children, including infections and many chronic conditions. They have also been used to treat animals. Great success has been claimed with treating allergic conditions, such as hayfever, with homoeopathic remedies, as well as stress-related problems such as migraine and eczema.

Remedies may be given in hospital, both before and after operations, to counteract any effects of anxiety, shock and the anaesthetic, and to speed up healing. People treated homoeopathically appear to make a much more rapid post-operative recovery than those who have not had this treatment.

The therapy has a direct part to play in surgical emergencies, mechanical damage or dysfunction and other severe, acute problems, but only in the hands of suitably trained homoeopaths. Homoeopathy cannot cure certain mechanical problems, but can reduce the effects of trauma.

Treatment
The initial appointment might last for an hour or longer. Details of a person's temperament, likes and dislikes and health of immediate family members are noted. For example, it is considered important to know whether he or she prefers hot or cold weather, feels better or worse by the sea or in the mountains, whether mood can be changed by music, and his or her fears, hopes and achievements. Many of the questions asked may seem to have little relevance to the condition being treated, but to find a remedy it is necessary to build up a picture of the individual with an emphasis on his or her mental characteristics. Medical history is also recorded.

Once all important details have been elucidated, the practitioner will make a diagnosis and prescribe a single remedy. The remedy is chosen on the basis of a person's personality, physical symptoms, signs and modalities, that is, factors which either reduce or intensify symptoms.

The remedy is usually prescribed in tablet form, though it may be a powder, tincture, ointment or granules. A remedy will work with the body's natural healing force to help it achieve a state of equilibrium. It stimulates the body's own defences, or 'vital force', and may therefore aggravate the symptoms slightly before curing. It is at this stage that the practitioner may suggest changes in lifestyle, such as a change in diet, more rest and or exercise. Homoeopaths generally recommend that patients do not drink coffee, eat highly spiced food or peppermint, or use eucalyptus oil, camphor or menthol while having homoeopathic treatment, as any of these may antidote the effect of the remedy. (The restriction also includes the use of many proprietary toothpastes and mouth-washes.) At the following session, the practitioner will want to discuss what has happened since the previous appointment and to check how the remedy is working. It is difficult to say how many consultations will be required as each person is unique and each disease affects individuals in different ways. With long-term conditions such as rheumatism, patients need to be monitored over many months, and repeat prescriptions or different remedies might be given if improvement stops or new symptoms develop.

Many newly qualified practitioners set up in partnership in a clinic, or practise where there is a senior practitioner to advise them. A growing number of registered homoeopaths now work with GPs, particularly in fundholding practices.

Training

Medically Qualified Homoeopathic Practitioners

The Faculty of Homoeopathy

The education programme of the Faculty is primarily intended to train orthodox physicians, veterinary surgeons, dental surgeons and pharmacists in the practice of homoeopathic medicine, provided that they have qualifications which can be registered with the General Medical Council, the Royal College of Veterinary Surgeons, the General Dental Council and the Royal Pharmaceutical Society, respectively.

There is a full-time six-month postgraduate course, known as the Long Course, to instruct doctors who have been qualified for a minimum of two-and-a-half years. There is also a part-time faculty postgraduate course, divided into seven modules.

The course comprises lectures on homoeopathic *materia medica*, philosophy, repertorisation and research. At the end of the course an exam is set comprising 10 case histories of not more than 1,000 words each and two exam papers on the principles and practice of homoeopathy, *materia medica* and therapeutics. In addition there is a clinical exam. The fee is currently (1994) £2,500.

Non-Medically Qualified Homoeopathic Practitioners

The British School of Homoeopathy

The School runs a professional four-year, part-time training course, which it is currently (1994) applying to register for university degree status. There is no fixed age limit for those who wish to register for the course. The minimum educational requirement is two A levels, but this requirement may be waived for those over the age of 25.

The principal areas in which a student will be expected to reach a measurable level of competency are: the principles of homoeopathy; human anatomy and physiology; pathology; homoeopathic diagnosis; and homoeopathic *materia medica* (knowledge from a homoeopathic reference book on remedies). The student will also be expected to demonstrate competence in the treatment and management of cases, the provision of treatment and evaluation of success. He or she will also need to demonstrate appropriate levels of competency in the management of a practice, cooperation with other professions, research and efficient communication with patients and colleagues.

The first three years comprise 11 weekend training seminars, structured and guided home study of 15–20 hours each week, written homework and basic clinical training. The fourth year consists of further weekend seminars, supervised clinical training and project work.

The fees for the first academic year are £1,150. The total outlay required for the course will not, therefore, be less than £4,600.

The College of Homoeopathy

The College provides a course which may be taken either part or full time. The syllabus, which is divided up into units, is as follows: clinical and clinically related learning; homoeopathic philosophy; homoeopathic practice and methodology; *materia medica*; human sciences; practitioner development; tutorials and consolidation sessions; and complementary studies. All units are clinically related in differing degrees. Variations in the balance between theoretical and practical aspects reflect the increasing importance of clinical experience and professional development as the course programme progresses.

The full-time programme comprises a minimum of three years and involves 21 hours' (three days) attendance per week with regional tutorial attendance of 12 or more hours a week. The total contact hours will be a minimum of 1,680 hours.

The fees for the full-time course are currently (1994) £2,988 which will mean a total outlay of not less than £8,964.

The part-time course comprises a minimum of four years' study and involves attendance at 11 weekend sessions of two full days per year, 21 hours per week of home study, regional tutorial attendance and progressively intensified clinical attendance throughout the course. The total contact hours will be at least 638 hours.

The fees are currently (1994) £1,350 per year which will mean a minimum outlay of £5,400.

The London College of Classical Homoeopathy

The college offers both a four-year full-time course and a four-year part-time course.

The full-time course offers a very thorough understanding of homoeopathy through a continuous stream of in-depth study. Although it is structured as a four-year course it is possible for students to complete their studies and qualify in three years. The fourth year gives the essential support in the early days of practice, providing a painless and successful transition from student to professional practitioner. For the part-time course, lectures are held on 13 weekends each year, grouped around term times, with tutorials arranged locally whenever possible to ensure continuity of study and a point of contact for the student between each weekend. It is suggested that students add a minimum of 52 hours in tutorials each year between weekends. Approximately 15 hours of home study are required each week. Homework and assignments are given in each subject.

The syllabus for both the full-time and part-time courses is as follows: the philosophy of homoeopathy, with particular reference to Hahnemann's *Organon; materia medica;* human sciences (taught from an holistic viewpoint); psychology and psychotherapy; the history of homoeopathy; pharmacy; computer studies; and practical first aid.

Written exams are taken in philosophy, *materia medica* and human sciences in the fourth year.

Applicants should be over the age of 21 and have GCSE human biology. If under the age of 21, applicants should offer five GCSEs or three A levels.

Fees for the full-time course are currently (1994) £2,910 per year, making a total outlay necessary of not less than £11,640. Fees for the part-time course are £1,470 per year, making a total outlay necessary of not less than £5,880.

The School of Homoeopathy

Study starts with a foundation correspondence course, comprising twin study units and a summer school. Students who complete this stage may attend the School for additional part-time study. Attendance at the clinic is essential. There is also a period of in-service training under the guidance of a professional supervisor. The foundation course involves over 1,000 hours of study. The syllabus comprises an in-depth analysis of the philosophy and science of homoeopathy and a comprehensive overview of the *materia medica*.

The fee for the foundation course is currently (1994) £650.

The second and third years of the course consist of 10 three-day weekends at approximately monthly intervals. During the third year the student, under close supervision, will be expected to take the cases of, and prescribe for, 10 patients. The syllabus for the second and third years comprises in-depth discussions of the philosophy of homoeopathy, case analysis and the study of pathology and pharmacology.

The fee for the second and third years is currently (1994) £1,175 per year.

The fourth year consists of five extended weekend sessions, with the emphasis on further development of skills in case taking and analysis. The major focus is on in-service training under the guidance of an experienced supervisor.

The fee for the fourth year is currently (1994) £600. Total fees: £3,600.

Registering Organisations

The Faculty of Homoeopathy
Those who qualify as registered medical homoeopathic practitioners are entitled to register as members with the Faculty and to carry MFHom after their names.

The Society of Homoeopaths
The Society of Homoeopaths is the professional body for homoeopaths practising in the Hahnemannian tradition and it maintains a register of practising homoeopaths. Colleges which aim to train to the Society's standards are: The British School of Homoeopathy; The College of Classical Homoeopathy; The College of Homoeopathy; The College of Practical Homoeopathy; The London College of Classical Homoeopathy; The Northern College of Homoeopathic Medicine; The North West College of Homoeopathy; Purton House School of Homoeopathy;

The School for Advanced Homoeopathic Studies (postgraduate); The School of Homoeopathic Medicine (Darlington); The School of Homoeopathy; The Yorkshire School of Homoeopathy.

The courses run by these colleges usually last four years with the emphasis in the first three years on theory and the fourth year geared more towards more supervised, clinical practice. Practitioners are issued with a certificate of registration, following a site visit and peer review, and may use the initials RSHom after their names. The Society is currently (1994) seeking formal accreditation for the courses it recognises.

Case Study

Francis has been an homoeopathic practitioner for many years and trained at the College of Homoeopathy.

I became interested in homoeopathy because I was a successful patient. I had hepatitis and some years later was still not well. My dentist sent me to his brother, a practising homoeopath. I had not consciously heard of the word 'homoeopathy' but I went along to the man and after one remedy and being told to stop drinking coffee I was transformed. I picked up an old book in a second-hand bookshop and was so fascinated by it that I've now got a library of some 3,000 volumes on homoeopathy.

What I remember best about my training was the excitement! Homoeopathy made sense as a logical system, whether or not you believed it. And there was a lack of fear – we learnt to banish fear, fear of medicine and fear of the unknown. There was also the intensity. You needed to be a fanatic in devotion to study as there was an enormous body of knowledge to get to grips with. about 25 per cent of the face-to-face lecturing time was in conventional medical sciences and this had to be integrated into traditional homoeopathic learning. I think the most valuable element of the training was the intensive study of materia medica, *the properties of the medicines.*

After I finished training I moved about a bit. Initially I practised in Neals Yard in London. I then went to India on a planned course of study to gain more clinical experience. Then for two years I practised in Manchester. Subsequently I came down to London in 1988 and started a private practice in North London which is still going. I was invited to join Marylebone Health Centre, a progressive NHS practice, where I worked for three years. In November 1993 I started practising in North London in a fundholding practice which means the practice has more control over its expenditure.

When I see patients for the first time, the consultation takes at least an hour – longer if needed. I explain what homoeopathy is, if they are new to it, and give out leaflets. I think it's important to begin by letting patients talk. I'll say 'and is there anything else?' two or three times to make sure everything has been said that needs saying. After this I ask detailed questions about how problems are experienced – I need to know my patients, to know their reactions to a range of natural phenomena such as the weather, their sleep patterns, hot and cold temperatures, food desires, aversions, upsets, menstrual cycles, and so on. If they tell me about the present, I find a way of introducing their history; it's about the facts and how they react to things in their lives. I might then give a physical examination and follow with a prescription. This might vary from a single dose to doses up to three times a day for a month. If a patient is taking conventional medicine which antidotes, there's more likely to be the need for frequent repetition of doses. I get emotional – full of joy – when patients get better, and they often get better even when they've been told that conventional medicine can do nothing for them.

I think standards in homoeopathy are the most important element today. There must be high standards in basic and continuing education, and monitored standards of practice. When State registration happens, the standards must not be diluted. Another important factor is the cost-effectiveness of the discipline. The remedies, for instance, compare very favourably in price with conventional medicines. And removing the need for non-urgent surgery also saves money.

8

Hypnotherapy

Definition and Principles

Hypnosis is a state of altered consciousness during which the unconscious mind, which controls autonomic bodily responses, becomes receptive to suggestion. Hypnotherapy, often referred to as the art of suggestion, uses hypnosis to tap into the unconscious to achieve behavioural change. The therapy is not physically addictive and no drugs are used.

History

Hypnosis has been practised for thousands of years; various forms of suggestion were known to the ancient Greeks and Egyptians.

The father of modern hypnotherapy was Dr James Braid (1795–1860), a Scottish surgeon who worked in Manchester and who used hypnotism on patients in the operating theatre. In 1843 he published *Neurypnology* which argued that the trance state was genuine. He suggested that the combined state of physical relaxation and altered conscious awareness entered into by patients should be called hypnotism, from the Greek *hypnos*, meaning sleep, as it appeared to the observer that they were in a sleep-like state.

In 1893 a BMA committee reported on hypnotism, stating that 'as a therapeutic agent, hypnotism is frequently effective in relieving pain, procuring sleep and alleviating many functional ailments'. In 1955 a second BMA report on hypnotism approved the use of hypnosis for the treatment of psychoneuroses and for the relief of pain. It also recommended that all doctors and medical students should receive adequate training in its application.

Hypnotherapy Today

In recent years there have been many criticisms of the way in which the therapy is practised, partly owing to lack of knowledge about the discipline and the limited number of reputable hypnotherapeutic organisations.

There are no restrictions in the UK on the practice of hypnotherapy and there is no statutory control. Currently there are about 80 hypnotherapy organisations, many of them offering courses of a few days only. Anyone can place an advertisement offering hypnotherapy; certificates and diplomas can be obtained without any legal check; anyone can set up a training school. It would seem to be very important for the profession to be regulated and for it to achieve statutory recognition in the near future.

Conditions Used For

The therapy has had many successes in the treatment of physical conditions where there is probably a strong psychological element. For example, psychosomatic illnesses such as hysterical paralysis or kleptomania, or conditions caused by stress such as migraines, nail-biting, bed-wetting, eating disorders and skin problems (eczema and psoriasis), as well as problems in the gastro-intestinal tract such as colitis which are thought to be stress related. Hypnotherapy has also proved effective in the the treatment of insomnia and anxiety and in treating phobias, such as fear of spiders, exams, heights or flying, and addictions and dependency states, such as alcoholism, smoking and gambling. In dentistry, the technique is used for analgesia, especially when patients are allergic to anaesthetics.

Hypnotherapy cannot help directly with purely physical illnesses, though it can provide pain relief. No reputable hypnotherapist, however, would remove pain completely without consultation with a patient's GP, as pain is a warning of a possibly serious dysfunction, such as a tumour. It has also been suggested that hypnotherapy should not be used for certain states of depression, such as symptomatic or manic depression, as the stillness, inertia and introversion of hypnotherapeutic techniques are very similar to the symptoms shown in depression.

Treatment

At the first session, the hypnotherapist will take a detailed history of the subject, paying particular attention to the symptoms presenting and also to past treatments by other practitioners. Subjects should be given a full explanation of hypnosis and what the practitioner thinks is likely to happen at subsequent sessions. It is very important to build up a rapport with those being treated, and intelligence and empathy are required to identify their needs.

Hypnosis is unlikely to be used at the first session but the subject may be tested for possible susceptibility to the treatment. At the second and subsequent sessions the subject, having been asked to sit comfortably or lie down, will be 'inducted' by the therapist, that is, put into a trance-like state, usually by being talked to quietly and having repeated suggestions made about being tired, needing to close the eyelids, etc. The subject may be asked to look at something such as a slowly turning wheel, which will increase the desire to close the eyes. The trance-like state induced by hypnosis helps a person to become more compliant, relaxed and open to suggestion. A person under hypnosis is not asleep and is aware of what is happening – the brain produces images but is too relaxed to think coherently. While in this state the subject may be guided by the therapist to view problems from a more positive perspective, to bring forgotten memories back to consciousness, and to gain insight into past and future behaviours.

The therapist may implant suggestions which may be triggered after the subject has come out of the trance, but research has demonstrated that it is impossible to make anyone do anything against his or her moral or religious convictions while under hypnosis. Contrary to what is commonly believed, the patient never loses control and some part of the mind is always aware of what is being said and done. Some therapists use negative suggestions, for instance, 'You won't feel sick next time you board an aircraft'; it is more usual, however, to adopt a positive approach, such as 'You will feel well when you board an aircraft'.

Once the therapist considers the subject has had enough treatment for the session, he or she is gently returned from the hypnotic state to normal consciousness. Discussion then takes place and the hypnotic state is examined to inform and enhance future therapy sessions. Many subjects are taught how to induce self-hypnosis to help with relaxation, and the therapist may provide tapes to help.

The first session may last for up to two hours. Second and subsequent treatment sessions usually last for up to an hour. Simple techniques for relaxation or dealing with minor phobias may require only two or three sessions but complex problems may require many more treatments.

Most hypnotherapists are in private practice and work either on their own or in a group practice, but there is increasing scope for work in hospitals, especially in clinics dealing with particular problems, for instance, post-surgical rehabilitation.

Training

The National Association of Counsellors, Hypnotherapists and Psychotherapists Training Faculty

The training faculty offers a course which is designed to provide a thorough background and knowledge of counselling skills, hypnosis and psychotherapy. Students must be at least 25 years old and have five GCSEs, or O levels, and two A levels. Mature candidates who are unable to fulfil these criteria are asked to demonstrate their ability and commitment to undertake the course.

The course is divided into three parts of four, ten and four weekends, comprising a total of 18 weekends or 216 hours. Extensive home study is required during the second and third stages.

The course aims to give prospective therapists a thorough background in all the skills they are likely to need to work with clients in a non-judgemental, empathic and eclectic way. The syllabus includes counselling skills, hypnosis and its therapeutic applications, psychotherapy, psychology, basic anatomy and physiology, neuro-linguistic programming (NLP) and practice management.

The cost of each weekend is currently (1994) £95 and there are additional supervision costs for the year which come to £150, necessitating a total outlay of at least £1,860.

The registering body of the training faculty is the National Association of Counsellors, Hypnotherapists and Psychotherapists (see p. 81).

The National College of Hypnosis and Psychotherapy

The College offers training in hypnotherapy through part-time courses held at weekends in London, Cheshire and Glasgow. All applicants seeking enrolment must either have a university degree or equivalent, or a professional qualification such as SRN, CQSW, or two A levels, or GCSEs or O levels in a least five subjects. Those without formal qualification must demonstrate interest, enthusiasm and life experience appropriate to helping others by means of therapy and show aptitude and potential for study.

The training is in three stages: Stage 1, the foundation course, aims to give students a knowledge of hypnosis and to train them to be efficient in inducing the hypnotic state, and in its management, with the emphasis on practical training. It involves 40 hours of attendance, usually spread over four weekends, at one of the tuition venues. Stage 2 covers theories of psychotherapy and additional techniques in hypnotherapy. The syllabus for this course requires students to attend for some 60 hours, usually spread over six weekends. Stage 3 leads to the award of the Diploma in Hypnotherapy and Psychotherapy, upon successful completion of a dissertation and a practical examination. The period of attendance is four weekends, comprising a total of some 40 hours.

The fees for Stage 1 are currently (1994) £399.50, plus an exam fee of £15; for Stage 2, the anticipated fees are £705 plus an exam fee of £75; for Stage 3 the anticipated fee is £470 plus a dissertation fee of £50. The anticipated outlay will therefore be a minimum of £1,714.50.

The registering organisation of the College is the National Register of Hypnotherapists and Psychotherapists (see p. 82).

The National School of Hypnosis and Psychotherapy

The School provides a course in hypnosis which is divided into two parts. Students are taught to develop their skills in the clinical arts of observation, hypnotic inductions and the formulation of indirect suggestion to enable them to become practising hypnotists. They are also taught an understanding of the dynamics of unconscious processes in behaviour, to have a high regard for the unique life experiences of each individual and to treat the whole person, not merely the symptoms.

Part I consists of four weekends (approximately 72 hours) of class work, together with approximately four hours of homework each week. Part II consists of over 72 hours of classwork and additional homework. Students submit a total of three dissertations during Part II to indicate their understanding of the subject matter. The final diploma exam takes place approximately one month after completion of Part II and consists of two days of formal exams, one day of which is practical work and the second a written exam of four papers. There is an obligatory period of one year of post-diploma clinical supervision, together with a non-obligatory advanced diploma course, consisting of four weekends, for graduates wishing to proceed to full membership of the Central Register of Advanced Hypnotherapists (see p. 81) and entry to the ICM's British Register of Complementary Practitioners (Hypnotherapy) (see p. 15).

The Proudfoot School of Hypnosis and Psychotherapy

The School provides a suite of three courses entitled Hypno-NLP which take place in three separate steps of one week each. The first is on hypnosis and includes sessions on learning about hypnosis, fears of hypnosis, the nature of hypnosis, the nature of suggestion, induction techniques, focusing, instantaneous hypnosis, the misuse of hypnosis and how to start up. The second course is on hypnotherapy and includes hypnotherapeutic techniques, regression techniques, gestalt and dreamwork. The third course is on neuro-linguistic programming (NLP) and includes calibrating, changing a personal history, eliciting submodalities, new behaviour generating, pacing and leading and six-step retraining. The length of each course is 50 hours.

The fees for each course are £395.

The School is affiliated to The Association of Professional Therapists (see p. 81).

Registering Organisations

The Association of Ethical and Professional Hypnotherapists
The Association was formed to meet the need for an association with a clearly defined Code of Ethics. All members sign a declaration that they will at all times place the welfare of the patient above all other considerations, and that if it is considered that the patient would benefit from the services of another practitioner, he or she will be so informed. Membership, designated with the letters MAEPH, is open to graduates of courses run under the auspices of the organisation. A register of members is maintained and is available on receipt of an SAE.

The Association of Professional Therapists
Requirements for membership, designated by the letters MAPT include one of the following: a diploma from the National College of Hypnosis and Psychotherapy; a diploma from the National School of Hypnosis and Psychotherapy; an advanced diploma from the Proudfoot School of Hypnosis and Psychotherapy. The Association would normally expect to see a minimum of 130 hours' classroom training. It is an independent, non-profit-making organisation and is not attached to any college or training institution.

The Central Register of Advanced Hypnotherapists
This is the professional association for students and graduates of the National School of Hypnosis and Psychotherapy. Membership is designated with the letters MCRAH.

The National Association of Counsellors, Hypnotherapists and Psychotherapists
This is the professional association of therapists who have trained with the National Association of Counsellors, Hypnotherapists and Psychotherapists Training Faculty. Members are designated with the letters MNACHP. The Association is a member of the Association of Hypnotherapy Organisations within the British Complementary Medicine Association.

The National Register of Hypnotherapists and Psychotherapists

This is the professional association of therapists who have trained with the National College of Hypnosis and Psychotherapy. All members of the Register, designated by the letters MNRHP, are required to adhere to a code of ethics and to carry appropriate insurance. A nationwide system of referral for members of the public seeking a reputable therapist is offered, together with an annual Directory of Practitioners. The Register provides in-service training and a national system of supervision for members. It provided the initiative behind the Institute of Complementary Medicine's British Register of Complementary Practitioners (Hypnotherapy) (see p. 15).

9

Meditation and Yoga

Meditation: Definition and Principles

Meditation is practised with the aim of reaching a tranquil state
to refresh the mind and relax the body. It is not a technique or a
way of thinking but rather a process of contemplation or concentration. For example, one might contemplate a *mandala* (a
spiritual painting in geometric form) or concentrate on a
mantram (a sacred word or phrase) to reach a meditative state.
The powers of concentration and control of thought processes
are used to calm the mind and slow down bodily processes.
Many consider it a way of achieving spiritual enlightenment.

Meditation: History

Meditation has been practised for thousands of years by many
cultures, particularly in the East, in India and much of Asia, but
also in the West.

Meditation Today

The importance of meditation for achieving a balance between
mind and body and for ensuring good health is being discovered by practitioners of conventional medicine and other

complementary and alternative therapies. There is growing interest in the discipline in the UK.

Conditions Used For

Research has shown that breathing and brain activity are enhanced and blood pressure and heart and pulse rates are lowered by meditation. It would appear that susceptibility to stress-related disorders and mental problems are substantially reduced by its practice.

Method

Meditation is not easy, as it requires contemplation, concentration, persistence and time. It is best not to eat or drink for half an hour prior to meditating. Choose a room where you cannot be interrupted. Some people lie down and close their eyes, but you should be alert and in control, so it might be better to sit comfortably upright with eyes open and hands resting in the lap.

The aim is to stop troublesome or stimulating thoughts. This is perhaps most easily achieved by focusing on one neutral or pleasing thought to the exclusion of all others. Sometimes a device is used to help, such as concentrating on breathing or using a mantra or focusing on an object. Meditation should be undertaken for 10 minutes or more at a time. By reducing the flow of information and sensations mental responses are also reduced. Attention is directed inwards, beyond mental activity, to an inner calm and an awareness of an inner self.

Meditation: Training

The School of Meditation

The School teaches meditation, brought from a tradition in India, on an individual basis at one teaching session only, lasting one-and-a-half hours. Meditation is then practised twice a day, with two guidance sessions at the school in the first week followed by weekly half-hour visits for about two months.

Everyone who learns to meditate is asked to make a donation to assist with the costs of the School. This is normally set at one week's net income but individual circumstances are taken into consideration. The minimum contribution is £50 and the maximum £200.

Transcendental Meditation

Transcendental meditation is taught at 80 centres throughout the UK by teachers trained by Maharishi Mahesh Yogi in a course of seven systematic steps.

1. Introductory presentation (60 minutes).
2. A more detailed explanation of the origin and mechanisms of the technique (45 minutes).
3. Personal interview with a teacher (15 minutes).
4. Personal instruction; learning the technique (90 minutes).
5. Instruction seminar 1 (90 minutes).
6. Instruction seminar 2 (90 minutes).
7. Instruction seminar 3 (90 minutes).

Yoga: Definition and Principles

Yoga, coming from a word in Sanskrit meaning 'union' or 'yoke', is an ancient Eastern method of spiritual, mental and physical training. There are many different kinds of yoga, such as Bhakti yoga, the way of devotion and union with the divine principle through religious devotion, and Karma yoga, the way of selfless action and service to others through work. The yoga method taken up in the West is Hatha yoga (from Sanskrit *ha*, 'sun' and *tha*, 'moon'). This is the physical expression of yogic practices through physical postures. It is a means of self-help towards physical and mental health and an holistic approach to self-development. It may be described as a science of self-knowledge or a journey of self-discovery. It is a practical philosophy, not a religion – though all the great religions echo its teachings.

Yoga: History

Yoga existed in India over 2,000 years ago. Originally it was known only to those who had abandoned worldly ways for mystical practices, and for many centuries was restricted to a small elite who lived apart in forests or caves. Teachers of the discipline worked out some of the yogic postures by watching and imitating the movements of animals.

There are many ancient texts devoted to the study of yoga, the best known of which is probably the *Bhagavad Gita* (*c.*300 AD), which teaches mainly Gnana, Bhakti and Karma yogas.

Hatha Yoga Today

In the 1990s many medical practitioners, as well as those who have had no medical training, are becoming increasingly interested in yoga with its emphasis on awareness and control of both mind and body. About half a million people in Britain now practise yoga regularly and there are some 5,000 teachers. There is, however, a shortage of qualified teachers in some parts of the country.

In 1983 the Yoga Biomedical Trust investigated the reactions of 2,700 people who practised yoga and were suffering from one or more of 20 different ailments. For each condition, over 70 per cent claimed that yoga had helped their condition to improve. Out of a total figure of 1,142 suffering from back pain, 98 per cent said their back pains had been alleviated, and of 834 people suffering from anxiety symptoms, 94 per cent said their symptoms had been alleviated by practising yoga.

Conditions Used For
The aim of therapeutic yoga is to promote and maintain healthy minds and bodies, although its practices are increasingly used to cure or alleviate disease. Yoga helps to reduce stress and control breathing. It has proved effective in controlling asthma, diabetes and reducing high blood pressure, and is beneficial for ME, heart disorders, bronchitis, multiple sclerosis, arthritis, lower back pain, menstrual and menopausal problems, constipation, headaches, muscular dystrophy, hypertension, hyperventilation and constipation. It can be extremely effective in cases of nervous debility and with mental conditions such as schizophrenia, depression and various phobias, as well as eating disorders and addictions. Yoga develops the ability to relax and is instrumental in providing greater strength, suppleness and better posture.

Method
The joints and muscles are kept strong by various exercises, while the respiratory system is developed and controlled by

breathing exercises which are seen to improve mental and emotional clarity. After a Hatha yoga session, participants should feel both physically and mentally relaxed, with no subsequent aches and pains from too much physical activity. Yoga practice should not be seen to be a chore or duty but as part of day-to-day living, leading to an enhanced life experience.

A yoga class usually lasts between one and two hours. No set patterns exist and a yoga teacher should tailor routines to suit each individual. Postures, known as *asanas*, are performed standing, kneeling, sitting or lying on the back or front. Each *asana* needs to be performed fully, by working on both sides of the body, that is, both right and left. For each *asana* there is a counter *asana*, so that, for instance, an *asana* performed to the right is followed by one to the left. Counter *asanas*, often expressed as counter poses, remove the negative effect of the previous *asanas* and so help to maintain the physiological and psychological balance during the practice. They work in the opposite direction to the previous *asanas*, but in a more gentle, less vigorous, way. Most *asanas* work on the spine to keep it supple. At intervals, deep relaxation exercises are taught, as well as controlled breathing exercises, known as *pranayama*. The philosophy of yoga is usually taught, which includes learning about the 'eight limbs' of yoga: *yamas* (restraints), *niyamas* (observances), *asana* (posture), *pranayama* (breathing control), *pratyahara* (sense withdrawal), *dharana* (concentration), *dhyana* (meditation) and *samadhi* (heightened awareness). These are considered essential to the yoga way of life and health.

Yoga: Training

Traditionally, yoga is taught by a *guru* (teacher) to disciples. Yoga classes differ widely and there is no one institution which supervises teachers. The training needed to qualify as a yoga teacher may vary from a few weeks to two or three years, preceded by several years of regular practice. Yoga postures and breathing are effective only if practised regularly. Practise is a major requirement for teachers who should also have a knowledge of anatomy and physiology as well as a thorough training in their own particular branch of yoga.

The British Wheel of Yoga

The British Wheel of Yoga offers a two-year teaching diploma, comprising 150 hours of tuition. Students should have completed at least two years regular attendance with an approved yoga teacher before starting training.

The syllabus covers the practice and teaching of Hatha yoga techniques (including *kriyas*, *mudras* and *bandas*); relaxation and meditation, and basic anatomy and physiology. Theoretical study includes four set books: the *Bhagavad Gita*, the *Upanishads*, the *Yoga Sutras of Pantanjali* and the *Hathayoga Pradipika*. The syllabus also covers the area of professional studies, that is, learning about how to teach and planning courses and lessons.

The diploma course may be tutored privately, which means the teaching venue, hours studied, length of the course and fees are determined by the tutor. Courses may include a weekly attendance of two hours, a whole day once a month, or a weekend once a month. The course is also taught under the aegis of adult education authorities and a distance learning course is also available.

Iyengar Yoga Institute

Teachers' training courses are held for the three grades of introductory, intermediate and advanced teaching certificate. The training courses cover the techniques of teaching yoga: accuracy of instruction; demonstration; observation and adjustment; and control of the class. Teachers are expected to be familiar with the order, understanding, progression and application of postures, as well as with breathing techniques and relaxation. There are written papers on anatomy, philosophy and the therapeutic aspects of yoga.

The cost of the teacher training courses is currently (1994) £100 per term.

Viniyoga Britain

A foundation certificate course in yoga is provided with the aims of understanding yoga as a practice, philosophy, tradition, and as a tool for personal change. The course is over a period of one to two years, comprising four weekends and a minimum of 50 hours study. Topics covered are yoga practice, yoga sutra and related texts, the origins of yoga, asana, pranayama, ayurveda, the transmission of yoga from East to West and Sanskrit.

The weekend workshops currently (1994) cost £65 per weekend (excluding accommodation).

There is also a practitioner programme with the aim of providing an in-depth study of yoga as a practice, philosophy, tradition, tool for change in self and others, and as a complementary therapy. The course lasts for a minimum period of 450 hours over four years and is in yearly cycles of six residential weekend workshops, one six-day residential retreat and 12 hours of individual lessons. Prospective students will have taken the foundation course.

The syllabus comprises yoga practice, yoga sutra and related texts, origins of yoga, asana, pranayama, observation in asana and pranayama, therapy, yoga teaching, Sanskrit and the human system.

The cost of the residential workshops is currently (1994) £105 per weekend.

Yoga for Health Foundation
The Foundation runs a preliminary study course in yoga, lasting for about a year, which involves regular home study and test papers. There are four residential weekends. The three main parts of the syllabus are as follows:

The Philosophy and Psychology of Yoga. This covers the development of the yoga concept of a 'spiritual physics' and its application today.
The Anatomy and Physiology of Yoga. The yoga concept of body energy and control, plus contemporary medical anatomy and physiological understanding.
Pranayama and Asana. A study of Hatha yoga concepts.

The cost of the course is currently (1994) £340. Also offered is a foundation course in remedial yoga, costing £285.

The Yoga Biomedical Trust
The Trust offers a three-year, part-time yoga therapy diploma course which trains already qualified yoga teachers to become professional yoga therapists able to work in general practices, hospitals and holistic health centres. Prospective students should have a teaching qualification issued by an accepted school of yoga (or its equivalent), and a knowledge of anatomy

and physiology up to the level of the British Wheel of Yoga Teachers' training course (see p. 88) is required. They should also be practising yoga regularly themselves and have a commitment to developing their own understanding and experience of yoga.

There are 12 weekend sessions which concentrate primarily on medical foundations. There are also specialised courses on specific health problems which take place between two and five days and cover both theory and practice. The syllabus includes: anatomy and physiology in relation to common ailments and yoga therapy; methods of therapy used in various schools of yoga; practical application of yoga therapy in a range of patient conditions; relating yoga therapy to conventional medical treatment and other complementary therapies; patient assessment; consultation and counselling; record keeping; ethics and standards; clinic organisation and management; physical requirements; marketing; the law; opportunities for practice; general practices; hospitals; holistic health centres; schools; adult education authorities; special needs centres; research projects; and working from home.

Preparation of at least four case studies a year is required, including records of individual consultations, progress in classes and effects on health.

10

Naturopathy

Definition and Principles

Naturopathy is a philosophy, science, art and practice which aims to encourage health by both stimulating and supporting the body's inherent power, the *vis medicatrix naturae* (the healing power of nature), to maintain or regain health and balance. It is an holistic approach to health rather than a specific therapy and emphasises a way of life which is in harmony with nature.

Naturopaths see themselves as inducing health rather than curing disease; in fact, they never claim to cure, only treat, and stress the importance of disease prevention. They believe that only nature can cure. The discipline is based on four principles: (a) that the individual is unique; (b) that it is more important to establish the cause of the condition than to treat the symptoms; (c) that individuals have the power to heal themselves; and (d) that there is a need to treat the whole person and not just the area of the body affected.

It is claimed by naturopaths that the body will always strive towards equilibrium (health), but that the equilibrium can be disturbed by an accumulation of toxins. It is believed there are four distinct aspects of the healing process: (a) the self-healing mechanisms of the body known as *homoeostasis*; (b) the capacity of the organism to activate its self-healing mechanisms in response to treatment, known as *heterostasis*; (c) that disease is a manifestation of the body's inherent power applying itself to remove obstructions to the normal functioning of organs and tissues; and (d) that there is a tendency for the organism recovering from chronic disease to pass through more acute phases, a process known as the Law of Cure.

History

The philosophical basis of naturopathy is ancient. It can be said to date back to Hippocrates (*c.*460–375 BC), the 'father of medicine', who laid down the principle of 'first do no harm'. He maintained that good health is based on eating and exercising in moderation, and that disease, which he believed occurred as the result of an incorrect balance of humours in the body, should be treated in accordance with natural laws. He claimed that only nature heals, provided it is given the opportunity to do so; that, perhaps surprisingly, disease is an expression of purification, and fasting, the controlled abstinence from food, is beneficial because it allows the body to deal with the disease only rather than the additional process of digestion.

The term 'naturopathy' dates from 1895 when John Scheel, a German doctor practising in the USA, used it to describe his methods of treatment involving hydrotherapy and 'hygienics'. Seven years later, Benedict Lust, also practising in the USA, applied this word to a combination of natural therapies which set out to 'raise the vitality of the patient to a proper standard of health'.

Naturopathy Today

In the UK in 1990, a Commission on Naturopathic Medicine, entitled 'Report of the Commission on Naturopathic Medicine', sponsored by the General Council and Register of Naturopaths, drafted a definition of naturopathic medicine, its philosophy and practice. In it, the following therapies were defined as of primary importance in the naturopathic treatment of disease: (a) nutrition and dietetics; (b) fasting; (c) structural adjustments (massage or manipulative therapies); (d) hydrotherapy; (e) healthy lifestyle; and (f) education. The Commission also accepted that specialised therapies which are naturopathic in principle and practised by those qualified to do so may be considered complementary to the above methods. The therapies considered acceptable include osteopathy, chiropractic, relaxation techniques, herbal medicine, nutritional biochemistry and homoeopathy.

There are currently (1994) around 275 registered practitioners in the UK.

Conditions Used For

Naturopathy is said to be very effective against degenerative diseases such as arthritis and emphysema (chronic lung disease). It is used widely in digestive disorders, such as colitis and gastritis, and bronchitis, and has helped people with stomach ulcers and various forms of inflammation. Using naturopathic techniques is said to speed recovery in cases of sore throats, colds, influenza, diarrhoea and rashes. Naturopathy also helps with anxiety and tiredness and is thought to be highly successful in helping to prevent disease in bodily tissues and organs such as the lungs, kidneys and heart. It has been used successfully both to treat and prevent problems occurring with older people.

It should be noted, however, that a well-established acute infection is unlikely to respond to naturopathic treatment and naturopathy has no place in the immediate treatment of medical or surgical emergencies or severe trauma.

Treatment

Naturopaths treat each person and each case as unique. They take physical, emotional, biochemical and social circumstances into account.

At the initial session, a very thorough physical examination and questioning, usually lasting well over an hour, will be undertaken. This may include blood tests, urine analysis and X-rays. There may be an inspection of hair, nails, skin and mucous membranes of the mouth and tongue, as well as a routine inspection of the heart, pulse, lungs and blood pressure. The spinal joints and other parts of the musculoskeletal system may be checked to ensure they are in proper working order. Questions may include how the person is affected by the weather or by different times of the day, in what sort of areas they live and work, what types of event make up a daily routine, their eating habits, sleep patterns and physical factors such as menstrual cycles, bowel movements and frequency of urination. A person's mental and emotional state has to be considered very carefully as it is suggested that, for example, feelings of hate, self-pity, worry and fear produce poisonous toxins.

Diagnosis is concerned with establishing reasons for the symptoms and cause of the illness, as well as assessing the capacity of the individual's inherent power to restore the body to its functioning equilibrium. Treatment consists of finding ways for natural healing to take place by ridding the body of toxins and accumulated waste products and trying to ensure the underlying cause of the disease does not recur.

A naturopath would claim there is no point in suppressing the symptoms. For example, if there is a raised body temperature, it would be suggested that drugs should not be used to bring the temperature down. Inflammation is seen to have a purpose as a cleansing process, rather than just a phenomenon of infection. Disease generally is regarded as beneficial because it is suggested that it is the body's way of eliminating toxicity and restoring its natural balance.

Once the problem has been identified, the practitioner will suggest changes in lifestyle. For example, dietary changes, tailored to suit the individual, may be needed, as a person's innate power of healing cannot function effectively if he or she is not eating sensibly. In some instances, fasting may be necessary. There are several regimes, lasting from three to five days, with the patient ingesting only water or fruit juices or liquids and some vegetables. The purpose of fasting is to give the body a rest and to help in detoxification. Hydrotherapy treatment may be suggested, or the use of Bach Flower Remedies (see Chapter 13 pp 120 and 122). As far as psychology is concerned, naturopaths recognise the unity of the human organism and the indivisibility of body and mind. The psychological techniques practised recognise the body–mind concept and seek to release the psychological causative factors.

Under treatment, the general level of health should rise steadily, punctuated by 'healing crises' (the Law of Cure). The cure can only be said to have occurred when the body is in a fit enough state to make a recurrence unlikely. Once the original problem has been resolved and the patient maintains the lifestyle changes recommended, the likelihood of the problem recurring is significantly reduced.

Naturopaths aim to restore patients so they have no further need of treatment and are able to maintain their health by means such as whole food, fresh air, exercise, positive thinking, rest and hygiene.

An orthodox naturopath will support and stimulate the sick person's own vital powers, using only light, air, water, exercise, rest, nourishment and fasting. Drug therapy, toxic injections and vaccines are not used by naturopaths, but some practitioners may make use of other complementary or alternative therapies to help the body utilise its inherent power, provided the symptoms are not suppressed. Surgery is not a naturopathic treatment, though it is agreed that there are occasions when surgery may be necessary.

A naturopath will want to educate patients to take more responsibility for their own health. The importance of using natural therapies will be stressed. It is considered very important to explain to patients why disease occurs and what they can do to maintain the improved level of health received by naturopathic treatment. The number of consultations varies according to the individual and the underlying problem or problems.

Naturopaths may work in an outpatient clinic, a residential clinic or nursing home. Most work in private practice and see patients only by appointment. About 60 per cent of new practitioners start as assistants to established practitioners for at least part of the time before they set up on their own.

Training

The British College of Naturopathy and Osteopathy (BCNO)
The BCNO is the only college in Europe to provide a qualifying course in naturopathy, which comprises the BSc (Hons) degree in Osteopathic Medicine. The four-year, full-time course includes the study of nutrition, the principles and philosophy of natural therapeutics, clinical dietetics, applied natural therapeutics, psychology, psychosomatics and diagnosis. Successful students gain a Diploma in Naturopathy in addition to a degree in osteopathy. (For further details of this course, see Chapter 11, p.103.)

The British Naturopathic and Osteopathic Association
The two-year postgraduate modular diploma (ND) course in naturopathic medicine consists of 11 weekend modules spread

over a two-year period and is available to practitioners who are trained in primary health care disciplines, including osteopaths, chiropractors, medical herbalists, registered medical practitioners and others whose training is to an acceptable level. The purpose of the course is to provide a series of self-contained modules, beginning with an introduction to naturopathic medicine, which are taken individually, as and when desired by the practitioner, or as a series with the aim of building up course points towards the taking of the Diploma in Naturopathy external examination as set by the General Council and Register of Naturopaths.

Module 1: Introduction to naturopathic medicine. This includes: an introduction to the philosophy of naturopathy; the history and development of naturopathy; the principles and practice of therapeutic fasting; the principles and practice of clinical nutrition; the principles and practice of hydrotherapy.

Module 2: Nutrition. This is intended to give the student a detailed rationale and practical instruction in the therapeutic use of food and food constituents. It includes: an overview of the major nutrients and their functions; the physiology of digestion and absorption; the medicinal value of foods; the application of specific dietary regimes; the use of vitamin and mineral supplementation.

Module 3: Cardiovascular and respiratory conditions.
Module 4: Gastro-intestinal conditions.
Module 5: Musculoskeletal and neurological conditions.
Module 6: Allergic, immunological and endocrine conditions.
Module 7: Psychology and counselling.
Module 8: Genito-urinary system, gynaecology and obstetrics.
Module 9: Infections and dermatology.
Module 10: Paediatrics and geriatrics.
Module 11: Soft tissue and neuromuscular techniques.

Each of the modules will cover: a brief review of the anatomy, physiology and pathology of the area; an overview of the common conditions encountered; the naturopathic assessment of those conditions; the naturopathic treatment used, including fasting, general and specific diets, hydrotherapy, physical therapies, exercise, vitamin and mineral supplementation; and other relevant general or specific therapies.

Modules 1 and 2 are compulsory. From the remaining nine, the practitioner has to complete a minimum of seven in order to be eligible to sit the final examinations, which are based on the entire syllabus. Each module will follow a format that will enable practitioners to expand their scope of practice and immediately apply naturopathic treatment to the areas covered in the modules.

The cost of each module is £100.

Registering Organisation

The General Council and Register of Naturopaths

This is the governing and registering body for qualified naturopaths in the UK. It monitors educational standards for naturopathy and brings all people together who are properly qualified to engage professionally in the practice of naturopathy. It has nearly 200 members, who are designated by the initials MRN.

11

Osteopathy

Definition and Principles

Osteopathy, a complementary therapy to allopathic medicine, is the science of human mechanics, that is, a system of diagnosis and treatment which emphasises the structural and mechanical problems of the body, with special attention being paid to the spinal column.

An osteopath will treat each person differently, looking at the whole person, not just the symptoms. The aim of osteopathy is to correct problems in the body frame, making it easier for the body to function normally and thereby reducing the likelihood of problems occurring in the future. In seeking to maintain good health and prevent future problems, the osteopath's treatment plan may include advice on posture, diet, lifestyle and stress management.

History

Andrew Taylor Still was an American doctor who at one point also studied engineering. In the 1870s he developed osteopathy as a new system of treatment which emphasised the importance of the spine. He saw the human body as fitting together like a machine, and disease as being caused by spinal vertebrae slipping out of position. If the spine's function as a protective channel for nerves was impaired, the circulation of the blood was affected and ill health would result. Illness was seen as the result of blocked circulation.

Andrew Still expressed his beliefs in two fundamental principles: 'structure governs function' and 'the role of the artery is supreme'. The way to treat blocked circulation was, he claimed, by careful manipulation which would unblock the impediment to the blood flow and allow the body to cure itself.

The first formal teaching course was set up in Kirksville, Missouri, while the first school in the UK, the British School of Osteopathy (see p. 103), was founded in 1917 in London.

Osteopathy Today

Osteopathy is still governed by the principles laid down by Andrew Still in the nineteenth century. It is thought that our bodies depend on the operation of a finely tuned, complex system of bones and joints, controlled and moved by muscles and actuated by nerves. The bones and joints are surrounded by soft tissue containing the fluids of the circulatory system. Changes in the balance of this neuro-musculoskeletal system and its circulatory components may result in restricted flexibility and mobility, disturbance of the blood supply and malfunction of the nervous system. It is believed that the structure and function of the human body are completely interdependent; if the structure of the body alters the function immediately alters as well, and alteration of function eventually leads to an alteration of structure. Disease is seen as the result of these changes. Treatment not only increases the blood supply but also helps the lymphatic system to flush away impurities accumulated in the body's tissues. The movement of body fluids is regarded as vital to the normal state of equilibrium and their circulation is seen to be largely dependent on the nerves operating smoothly.

Osteopathy is mainstream in the USA and Canada. In the UK, The Osteopaths Act, which became law in July 1993, means that osteopathy will become formally recognised and regulated, on a par with medicine, dentistry, nursing and midwifery. When it comes into effect, probably in 1995, all osteopaths will come under the control of a new body, the General Osteopathic Council (GOsC), which will have a statutory duty to set and enforce standards of professional training and practice. It will seek for a uniform education policy, will maintain a register and deal with problems caused by sickness or unacceptable standards of competence and personal behaviour. Only registered practitioners will be allowed to describe themselves as osteopaths.

There are currently (1994) over 2,000 osteopaths in the UK registered with five different voluntary registers (which will all be replaced by the GOsC in 1995) treating over one million people a year.

In 1975 the General Medical Council sanctioned the referral of patients from doctors to osteopaths, provided they maintained clinical responsibility. Increasingly, patients are referred to an osteopath by their GP as the osteopathic approach becomes more widely accepted as an effective method, used either independently or in conjunction with medical treatment. The patient is, however, expected to pay a fee.

Conditions Used For
A wide range of disorders can be corrected using osteopathic treatment: joint pain and strain (including arthritis), back pain (including sciatica), frozen shoulder, cervical spondylosis, rheumatic conditions, sports injuries, asthma, dizziness and vertigo. Tinnitus, migraine, tension headaches, indigestion and respiratory problems respond well to treatment if they are the result of structural dysfunction. During pregnancy changes in posture may give rise to pain and discomfort and many women find relief with osteopathic treatment. Osteopathy can help after surgery, especially when the patient's body cannot adapt to the change in its mechanics. Osteopathy has also been used for hyperactivity in children, spasticity, Bell's palsy and menstrual problems.

Osteopaths accept they cannot cure most problems caused by genetic, environmental, bacteriological or toxic factors, though they do suggest that treatment might help to alleviate symptoms and lessen recurrences.

The treatment is not recommended for someone with osteoporosis when bones are brittle and joints are inflamed.

Treatment
At the initial session the practitioner will take a complete medical history and previous illnesses, injuries and other current treatments and lifestyle will be noted. Orthopaedic, neurological and circulatory examinations may be required as well as X-rays,

blood tests and urine analyses. The osteopath will make an assessment of the patient's posture and structural state and will conduct a detailed examination by touch, feeling the temperature and tone of the tissues and testing responses to movement. Restricted or excessive movements of the joints will be carefully noted and the soft tissues, muscles, ligaments and connective tissues will be examined. When all examinations have been completed and the diagnosis has been made, the osteopath will know whether manipulation is likely to help and if it would be safe. The suggested treatment programme may include advice on posture, diet, lifestyle and how to manage stress.

If manipulation is to be undertaken, the patient lies on a table in the best position for the osteopath to apply the desired amount of force and leverage through the hands. Osteopaths work with their hands using movements known as 'adjustments'. There is no standardised treatment for any condition and several techniques may be employed. For instance, the massage of soft tissue relaxes taut muscles and improves circulation, while gentle, repetitive, stretching movements improve joint mobility and reduce tension in surrounding muscles, at the same time improving blood circulation and fluid drainage. Fixed or malfunctioning joints may be released by manipulating the affected joints rapidly through their normal range of movement, known as the high velocity thrust technique, which often causes joints to click.

The treatment is seldom painful; usually patients find it pleasant and relaxing, though sometimes they may feel bruised and there may be a delayed response. Low back pain may be resolved after two or three 20- to 30-minute sessions but some chronic conditions benefit from regular treatment for up to ten sessions.

Cranial osteopathy, so named because it includes treatment of the head, is based on the concept of rhythmical involuntary movement being expressed through all tissues of the body. One of the places these movements are felt is through the bones of the skull. A trained practitioner can influence and assist this expression of health within the body in order to release mechanical restrictions and resolve any impediment to the self-healing process. The gentle nature of this treatment makes it particularly appropriate for babies and children, as well as the elderly.

Practising osteopaths are self-employed. Once qualified it is possible to set up independently, work in a healthcare centre or assist an established practitioner. Some osteopaths attend sports centres.

Training

The British College of Naturopathy and Osteopathy
The College offers a full-time, four-year programme leading to a BSc (Hons) in Osteopathic Medicine, validated by the University of Westminster.

The syllabus consists of a series of courses on the following:

Pre-clinical subjects. Biology, anatomy (including myology and neurology), physiology, pathology, osteopathic technique, neuromuscular technique, nutrition, principles and philosophy of natural therapeutics, principles and philosophy of osteopathy, soft tissue techniques and psychology.

Clinical subjects. Orthopaedics and traumatology, clinical dietetics, clinical osteopathy, clinical practice, applied natural therapeutics, diagnosis, osteopathic techniques, laboratory techniques, X-ray diagnosis, gynaecology, paediatrics and pharmacology.

Applicants must be at least 18 years of age and the minimum entrance requirements are two A levels in chemistry and biological science, or equivalent qualifications such as the Open University Science Foundation course, or science Access and foundation courses. Mature students are considered on an individual basis.

The annual fee is currently (1994) £5,300. The cost of the complete course will therefore amount to at least £21,200. An approved mandatory local authority grant is available.

The College is accredited by the General Council and Register of Osteopaths (see p. 106).

The British School of Osteopathy
The School offers a course leading to a BSc (Hons) in Osteopathy, validated by the Open University. There are two routes to the BSc: a full-time, four-year course or an extended

pathway, five-year course, first offered in September 1993. The course structure, clinical experience and exams are the same for both courses. The syllabus set out below is for the full-time, four-year course.

Year 1. The human organism: a detailed knowledge of its structure and function; the psychological and sociological contexts of health; practical aspects of osteopathy, including palpation and technique.

Year 2. Skills and understanding necessary for effective patient care; working as a supervised member of a clinical team; patient interviewing and examination skills; concepts underlying osteopathy; diagnostic clinical reassuring skills; skills in osteopathic technique; detailed knowledge of pathology; neuromuscular control mechanisms and other related areas.

Year 3. Management of patients in the clinic; refining and developing diagnostic and evaluative skills; increasing the range and depth of understanding human system failure; evaluating various approaches of osteopathy.

Year 4. Management of a list of patients; developing and evaluating approaches to ethical and related problems; acquiring and using up-to-date information from related disciplines, including orthodox medicine; preparing for future professional life.

A student will complete over 1,200 hours of clinical training during the four-year course.

To register for the course applicants must have five GCSE passes, two of which should be A levels in science subjects, preferably biology, chemistry or physics. Scottish applicants must have a minimum of five highers. Those who do not have the standard entrance qualifications may be required to complete a bridging course, Module 1 in physical sciences and/or Module 2 in anatomy and physiology at the School.

The fees for the first year of the four-year course are £5,610, and fees over the four years total more than £20,000. An approved mandatory local authority grant is available which amounts to 15 per cent of the annual fee.

The cost of the part-time five-year, course is as follows: Year 1: £5,500; Year 2: £4,500; Year 3: £4,500; Year 4: £4,000; Year 5: £4,000, necessitating a total outlay of £22,500. No grant is available for this course.

The School is accredited by the General Council and Register of Osteopaths (see p. 106) and affiliated to the Osteopathic Association of Great Britain (see p. 107).

The European School of Osteopathy
The School offers a four-year, full-time programme leading to a BSc (Osteopathy) Hons degree, validated by the University of Wales.

The curriculum is divided into seven modules as follows:

Induction Module. Introducing the student to the broad sweep of osteopathy, its language, principles and practice.
Three Core Modules. The three major anatomical regions of the body are studied in depth, integrating the study of structure, function, malfunction and technique.
Parallel Module. This runs concurrently with the core modules and provides an opportunity for students to develop and refine their hands-on skills and clinical techniques.
Integration Module. This provides an opportunity to review information acquired in the pre-clinical part of the course with an emphasis on interdependence, integrity and interplay between body systems.
Clinical Module. Most of the time is spent learning in a clinical situation with adequate opportunity for classroom review and private study.

Students who wish to register for the course should have three GCSE or O level passes, and two A levels or Highers in sciences, preferably human biology, chemistry or physics; or two GCSE or O level passes and three A levels, or highers, two of which should be appropriate science subjects; or Baccalaureate with sufficient science content; or International Baccalaureate; or any suitable BTEC or equivalent OND, ONC, HND or HNC; or any other equivalent qualification, for example, Open University study in relevant subjects to one credit level or a pass from an established and appropriate Access course.

The fees for 1994 are £4,500 (plus a one-off payment of £340 for the University of Wales), so the minimum outlay would be £18,340. An approved mandatory local authority grant is available.

The School is accredited by the General Council and Register of Osteopaths (see p. 106).

The London College of Osteopathic Medicine

The College provides a year's intensive course in osteopathy. Applicants should be medical practitioners with more than six years' good postgraduate experience involving patient contact. On acceptance, an exam, the Part One Examination, assessing knowledge of musculoskeletal anatomy and neurology, is required, designed to provide intending trainees with a goal to work towards in their preparation for the course and an opportunity to assess their knowledge.

The course starts in mid-May. The first four weeks of the course are taken up with lecture demonstrations introducing the trainee to methods of diagnosis and treatment, the neurophysiology of pain perception, musculoskeletal dysfunction and postural and occupational adaptation.

From week five, trainees must attend six half-day sessions per week for 48 of the ensuing 52 weeks to train for a minimum of 800 hours. From week six, trainees will be allocated patients for at least five of their half-day sessions each week and will be responsible for their management. Progress is continuously monitored.

The final clinical competence exam comprises a three-hour essay paper followed by a clinical exam during which the candidate's abilities in diagnosis and treatment are assessed. Those who qualify are entitled to become members of the College and to have the letters MLCOM after their names.

The Part One Examination costs £100 and the course fee (1994–95) is £2,200.

The College is accredited by the General Council and Register of Osteopaths (see below).

Registering Organisations

The General Council and Register of Osteopaths (GCRO)

The GCRO, with 1,800 registered members currently (1994), monitors the education and practice of osteopaths. It establishes and maintains standards of osteopathic education by inspecting schools, accrediting courses and training external examiners who assess students from accredited courses for their clinical competence and safety. The courses provided by the four schools listed above have been accredited, and are regularly inspected, by the GCRO, which also registers all graduates of the schools who are permitted the letters MRO (Member of the Register of Osteopaths) after their names.

The Osteopathic Association of Great Britain

This is a professional association for practising osteopaths. It has over 1,000 members who are graduates of accredited training courses.

Case Study

Jeremy works in two osteopathic practices in London for four days a week.

Initially I had nothing to do with osteopathy. I did a degree in computer science, then went into general management, working with a company in business. I then worked for myself for a while in marketing and sales. One year I had a stand at the Festival of Mind, Body and Spirit. Next door to me was a stand doing 'touch for health', a way of improving health by muscle testing in order to assess the balance in the acupuncture meridians in the body. I did a week's course in that and decided I liked working with people. But I wanted a more comprehensive training. I investigated many different courses in many different branches of complementary medicine and decided that osteopathy had the right balance of physical and mental activity. I chose the European School of Osteopathy diploma course [now a degree course; see p. 105] because it was the only one that covered involuntary mechanism work, cranial osteopathy, at an undergraduate level at that time. That was my particular orientation. I found it much more challenging than a 'normal' degree course, because it made you really question your basic way of looking at things, your philosophy of life.

The main areas of the course – anatomy, physiology, pathology – are very similar to a degree in medicine. In addition, however, you practise palpation, getting information from your hands about tissue states in the patient's body, learning to feel for the normal and the abnormal. Students start off practising on each other and later on in the course work in the School's clinic.

107

I find that two or three days is enough time spent working in any one room, so I work in two different practices, four days a week, two days in each practice. That's quite enough because the work demands a great deal of concentration; it's very exhausting. In my two practices I probably see about 15 patients a day, around 60 a week. I start work around 9 o'clock and allow half an hour for each patient. Andrew Taylor Still talks about 'Find it; fix it; leave it alone', and my way of working is very much along those lines. I work with a minimal treatment model where I look very carefully and diagnose as precisely as I can. I treat the problem and then, as far as possible, leave it alone and let the patients heal by themselves. What gives me most satisfaction in my work is the wonder of observing changes in the body. You can watch dramatic shifts in people's health and sometimes shifts in their total way of being as they proceed through a course of treatment.

Osteopathy is becoming a more united profession – slowly. People have worked in their own way over a very long period of time and now they are having to find common ground and develop out of that. That is a painful but essential process, and I see one of the major ways of achieving this is with postgraduate education which is something I'm involved with. There's a committee being set up for continuing osteopathic development in education, made up of representatives of all the schools and different registers, and we are trying to coordinate a further education policy for osteopaths with the goals of MSc and other academic qualifications, because one thing we do lack in the profession is a research base. We are also looking at continuing professional education, which is one of the things the Osteopaths Act has made space for, something new in healthcare education in this country.

12

Reflexology

Definition and Principles

Reflexology is an alternative therapy involving pressure being applied to specific parts of either foot in order to affect another part of the body. Reflexologists regard the feet as 'mirrors' of the body, with the left foot representing the left-hand side and the right foot the right-hand side. The body is treated without the use of drugs or surgery and application of the therapy is unique for each person.

Although it is not known exactly how the treatment works, it is believed that as areas of the feet are connected to other parts of the body, natural healing may be promoted through these by 'energy channels'. Reflexology works on both emotional and physical levels and allows for not only symptoms but causes of the symptoms to be treated.

History

The basic methods of reflexology have been practised for several thousands of years. It was known to the indigenous peoples of Africa and America and practised in ancient China. But it was not until the beginning of the twentieth century that the therapy was introduced into the Western world. In 1913, an American ear, nose and throat surgeon, Dr William Fitzgerald, became interested in the possibility of treating organs through pressure points far from the organs themselves. He noted that pressure in specific parts of the body might have an anaesthetising effect on a related area, and his theory divided the body into ten equal, vertical zones, ending in the fingers and toes. In the 1930s Eunice Ingham, an American therapist, refined and developed Fitzgerald's techniques into reflexology as it is known today. She observed that congestion or tension in any part of the foot mirrors congestion or tension in a corresponding part of the body.

Reflexology Today

Reflexology was introduced into the UK in the 1960s, notably by Doreen Bayly, who studied under Eunice Ingham and set up a training school (see p. 112). Today the therapy is one of the most popular alternative therapies, although there have been very few studies undertaken to validate the efficacy of the treatment. However, many people attest to the benefits they have received, and most who receive treatment find the massage very relaxing.

A study carried out in January 1990 in a Manchester hospital indicated that reflexology might significantly reduce anxiety and stress. Out of a total of nine elderly patients, three received reflexology treatment, three counselling and three no treatment other than the standard nursing care available, for eight days running. Subsequently, those who had received reflexology treatment showed a marked decrease in anxiety while in those who had received counselling the decrease was much less significant. Those who had had no treatment reported no change. Of the 14 nurses who took part in the survey, 12 maintained that foot massage had proved to be a useful technique.

Currently (1994), there are around 5,000 reflexologists practising in the UK. Since the beginning of the 1990s there has been a noticeable increase in the rate at which new students are becoming practitioners and a corresponding increase in the number of new schools. Nicola Hall, Director of the Bayly School of Reflexology, says of the current situation:

At the present time there are an increasing number of reflexology training schools which can be confusing for people wishing to study the method. Further confusion is added by the fact that there are also a number of different reflexology associations or societies. With the growing interest in [reflexology] it is important that there is more unity between these different representative groups so that reflexology can be spoken for with one voice.

Conditions Used For

Although reflexology does not claim to be a 'cure-all', the treatment is used to alleviate a great many conditions such as acne, eczema, psoriasis, bronchitis, sinus conditions, constipation, diarrhoea, disorders of the gastro-intestinal tract, circulatory problems, depression, ear, nose and throat conditions, incontinence, back pain, kidney disorders, menstrual problems, hormonal imbalances, breathing disorders, stiffness, poor peri- pheral circulation, tension, stress and insomnia.

It is important to note, however, that reflexology treatment should not be given for phlebitis (inflammation of a vein) and thrombosis (blood clotting). With heart trouble and pregnancy, particular care is required but treatment can be given.

Treatment

At the first session, the practitioner will take a detailed medical history of the person about to receive treatment. The latter will be seated in a reclining chair, or massage couch, or comfortable chair with a foot rest, with legs raised and without shoes or socks. The feet will be carefully examined before treatment begins.

A specialised massage is given, with the side of the thumb pressed firmly on to a particular reflex point. To release the pressure, the thumb is pulled back with a slight circular movement; it should always be kept bent. Sometimes the fingers are used. If the area being massaged is out of balance, a tenderness will be felt in the foot as pressure is applied. Areas which are tender, indicating an imbalance, will receive extra massage. With any given treatment all areas of the feet should be massaged so that the body is treated as a whole.

A treatment session usually lasts for about three-quarters of an hour, with a recommended course of six to eight treatments. An improvement may be noticed after the first session. If, however, there is no change after three sessions, reflexology may not be helpful in the particular instance. Following treatment, a number of reactions may occur, such as the need to pass more urine, an increased number of bowel movements, skin rash or urine, an increased number of bowel movements, skin rash or sore throat and running nose; it is suggested that these reactions are due to the body striving to eliminate toxins. In nearly all instances there will be a significant reduction in stress.

Most reflexologists are self-employed and work either from home or from a room rented in a natural health centre or multitherapy clinic. Only a very few work in the NHS, but an increasing number of nurses and physiotherapists are training in reflexology and are allowed to use the therapy in hospitals as part of their job.

Training

Although usually there are no formal academic requirements, reflexology is a practical skill which demands some knowledge of biology, anatomy and physiology. Some of the recognised schools in the field are listed below, together with accounts of their training courses.

The Bayly School of Reflexology
The training offered by the School is made up of attendance at three weekend courses and a final exam with essential home study and practice between the courses. Courses are available in London, Birmingham, Edinburgh, Dublin, Leeds and Malvern in Worcestershire.

Introductory Course. Covers the theory and principle of the relationship which exists between the reflex areas of the feet and nerves, glands and blood circulation.
Advanced Course. Aimed at those students who wish to train to practise reflexology as a profession. There is a detailed look at the treatment of specific disorders, anatomy and physiology, the use and application of hand reflexology, and advice on how to set up as a practitioner. Students are required to submit case histories of their reflexology work which involves 60 hours of treatment. A period of at least two months must elapse after the Introductory Course before students may attend an Advanced Course. After attending Part I of the Advanced Course, a further two months must elapse before Part II may be attended. After a further two months students may attend an Examination Day.

Examination Day. This comprises a two-and-a-half hour written paper and a practical assessment lasting for about three-and-a-half hours.

The cost for all four parts of the course is currently (1994) £350.

The Bayly School is affiliated to the British Reflexology Association (see p. 116).

The British School of Reflexology

Courses are available in Nottingham, London, Harrogate, Bristol and Harlow in Essex. The minimum age of acceptance is 21. A four-part training course is provided. The student attends on an alternate monthly basis, with each course backed up by correspondence study.

Part I (basic course). The principles of holistic healing and the history of reflexology are studied, together with anatomy and physiology, and the student starts to develop the correct pressure and control of thumb and fingers when applied to the feet.

Part II (intermediate course). The respiratory system, the central nervous system, spine, brain, urinary system, reproductive system, circulatory and lymphatic systems are studied.

Part III (advanced course). This includes working on four specific cases and learning how to access the main reflex areas likely to be sensitive.

Part IV (examination course). All aspects of the practical work are examined. The second day comprises both practical and written exams.

The total cost of all four courses is currently (1994) £799.

Postgraduate courses are held regularly throughout the year as a means of furthering the medical knowledge of the practitioners.

The British School of Reflexology is affiliated to the Association of Reflexologists (see p. 116).

The Crane School of Reflexology

The School's course consists of approximately 50 hours of theoretical work and about 300 hours of home study, together with 150 hours of practical training which the student is expected to complete in approximately eight months. Courses are held in York, London, Birmingham, Bristol and Harlow in Essex.

Level 1. History and principles of reflexology; relaxation techniques; contra-indications and cross reflexes; respiratory system and heat-related areas; digestive system.

Level 2. Endocrine, reproductive and urinary systems (functional connection); musculoskeletal system (spine and related areas); cardiovascular (heart and circulation) and lymphatic system.

Level 3. How to conduct a complete professional reflexology treatment session; treating specific conditions with reflexology techniques; understanding the effects of medication on the human body.

Level 4. Examination day, comprising a written paper and practical exam.

The fees are currently (1994) £595 for the complete course.

The Crane School of Reflexology is affiliated to The Reflexologists' Society (see p. 116).

Lillian Stoltenburg School of Holistic Reflexology and Massage

The School provides a comprehensive training course in holistic reflexology, the duration of which is 10 months. The minimum age for acceptance is 20 and the selection process is by interview. There are 120 hours of lectures, guided practice and tutorials and individual tuition and supervised clinical experience. There is also written homework between tutorials. There are two exams, consisting of one two-hour written paper and a 90-minute practical. The course is taught over a period of nine weekends:

1. Origins and theory of reflexology; zone theory; introduction to anatomy and physiology.
2. The nervous system; theory and principles of holistic medicine.
3. The endocrine system; diagnostic techniques; basic counselling skills; energy balance; indications of some organ conditions shown on the feet.
4. The lymphatic system; twentieth-century epidemics; reflexology and pain; meditations for the immune system.
5. The digestive system and urinary systems; nutrition workshop.
6. The respiratory system; cell biology; modern medicine and holistic health consciousness; the quality of thoughts and feelings; the chakra system in relation to reflexology.

7. The skeletal and muscular system; behaviour patterns; personal development of the therapist; Chinese philosophy of the feet.
8. How to set up a practice; first-aid for reflexologists; drugs and reflexology; information about the different registers and associations.
9. Practical and theoretical exams.

The fee for the complete course is £860.

The School is affiliated to the Institute for Complementary Medicine (see p. 15).

The Mary Martin School of Reflexology

The practitioners' training course is in three parts, with a total of 300 hours of practical and theoretical work and essential home study.

Part 1. Comprehensive instruction is given relating to the theory of reflexology and associated subjects. A working knowledge of the structure and function of the body is provided, together with an accurate location of the corresponding reflex areas of the feet. There is practical application of the therapy through guided practice sessions.

Part 2. Clinical experience is obtained using volunteer patients. There is evaluation of cases through class discussion and work with specific disorders. The effects of drugs are examined and there is discussion of good practitioner–patient relationships.

Part 3. This comprises written and practical exams and case studies.

The final assessment of a student is undertaken by an external examiner.

The cost of the course is currently (1994) £800.

The School is affiliated to the Association of Reflexologists and the Reflexologists' Society (see p. 116).

The Scottish School of Reflexology

The School has venues in Glasgow, Edinburgh, Dundee, Aberdeen, Newcastle and Manchester. The minimum age for acceptance on the course is 18.

Subjects include anatomy, physiology, pathology and reflexology theory. Students work in pairs for practical sessions and one tutor supervises five pairs of working students. Students are required to undertake five case studies of 12 treatments each. There are three exams: (a) a two-hour written paper on medical theory; (b) a two-hour written paper on reflexology theory; (c) a full-day practical assessment.

The fees for a full course are currently (1993–94) £690.

The Scottish School of Reflexology is affiliated to the Scottish Institute of Reflexology and Association of Reflexologists (see p. 117).

Registering Organisations

There are a number of registering organisations in the UK to which reflexology practitioners can apply for membership once they have completed their initial training and to which some of the reflexology schools are affiliated. The main ones in the UK are listed below.

The Association of Reflexologists
The Association has affiliated a number of training establishments and the organisation has a list of over 50 accredited practitioner courses. Members are designated MAR.

The British Reflexology Association
The Association, which is affiliated to the British Complementary Medical Association (BCMA) (see p. 14), acts as a representative body for persons practising reflexology as a profession and for students training in the method. Members are designated MBRA. The official teaching body is the Bayly School of Reflexology.

The Reflexologists' Society
The Society is affiliated to both the British Complementary Medical Association (BCMA) and the Institute for Complementary Medicine (ICM) (see pp.14 and 15 respectively), and is working to secure the future of reflexology in the UK and the EU. Members, designated MRxS, are required to have undertaken training lasting about nine months and to have done at least 200 hours' study and practical work, including home study, workshops and case histories.

The Scottish Institute of Reflexology
Membership is open to graduates of the Scottish School of Reflexology.

Case Study

Maureen trained over a period of nearly two years in reflexology with The International Institute of Reflexology. She works freelance, going to people's homes. She also works in a fitness centre one afternoon a week and for a charity with torture survivors.

I found the training in reflexology fascinating from the start, but you do wonder what on earth you're doing for quite a long time. You find it difficult to recognise what you're asked to look out for. For example, you are told you will feel a sort of grittiness under the thumb in areas where there is an imbalance, and you plod on, hoping that one day you will feel this, fearing you never will. Eventually, however, your hands get more experienced and you get used to the variety of feet you are presented with. Gradually you get to pick up energy levels and differences in texture of the surface and underlying areas of the skin. You need a lot of practice to become aware of what you are looking for, which is probably why the training is fairly long.

At the initial session, I talk to the client at length for up to an hour about his or her health generally, and lifestyle, and the specific problem brought to me. So I get a picture of the person I'm going to work with. Then I move on to the feet. At the first session I work all the reflexes to find out what's going on and whether that marries up with what the client has told me is the problem, or whether there are other things which seem to be out of balance. The second and subsequent sessions are much shorter and more specific, although I still keep an eye on the state of the body as a whole. I go straight into relaxation movements, which always begin a session, so that the client feels comfortable and at ease. I then briefly work the reflexes that were painful at the previous session. After that I work generally on the feet, making sure that the reflexes I'm not expecting trouble with are all right. I then come back to the painful ones. If the same reflexes are painful time after time I start to get a clear picture of what's going on in the client's body. I finish off each session with some relaxation movements.

I always get a buzz if after two or three sessions with a client who has had a chronic problem, perhaps for a very long time, he or she registers amazement that things are changing. Sometimes things change for the worse at first and some people I see get rather discouraged. But they don't always get worse; they may start to get better immediately and then there is great delight. Clients cannot believe that things have changed so quickly after such a long period of putting up with their problems and thinking that nothing can be done. This often happens.

What's really important for me is that the therapy is empowering to the client. Clients come often with years of passive acceptance of what orthodox medical advisers have told them they cannot or will not be able to do. With reflexology, they find they are expected to take an active part in the healing process, to be part of a partnership. This is very empowering for people, who change in all sorts of ways and not only in relation to their health. That's quite exciting!

I think reflexology will become, and is already becoming, more acceptable to the lay person and much better known. I've been practising since 1988 and I've seen quite a change during that time. When I first started, nobody knew what reflexology was. Nowadays, most people I meet have at least a vague idea of what the therapy is all about. Over a period of just five or six years it seems that people's perceptions have changed quite a lot. In some hospitals reflexologists now work on the chronically ill or the elderly. Work is also being done on treating people with AIDS, and nurses are being encouraged to use reflexology as an adjunct to their work.

13

Other Therapies

In this chapter, 10 therapies are covered in brief. Owing to the lack of space it is not possible to mention the very many other disciplines available. Further information can be obtained from books on holistic therapies to be found in local libraries, or through contacting the national organisations listed in Chapter 1.

Art Therapy

Art therapy is practiced in many parts of the world. By expressing themselves through the visual media of drawing, painting or modelling, clients may be helped to put into objective, and detach themselves from, strong negative emotions, and those with low self-esteem may be helped to gain confidence and a sense of achievement. The therapy releases buried emotions, and issues important to the clients are identified through the colours and shapes they produce. It has proved very effective with severely disturbed people who find it difficult to express their feelings verbally.

Clients are offered various art materials such as paints, crayons, charcoal, clays and plasticine, as well as paper, cardboard and old magazines and newspapers, all of which they are free to use as they wish. Art therapists interpret the meaning of the final product and hope to come to some understanding of their clients and thereby enable them to make new discoveries about their lives and selves.

Art therapy is used in prisons, mental hospitals and in schools for children with special needs. Within the NHS it is used mainly in psychiatric hospitals and day centres in the treatment of drug addiction and alcoholism as well as for HIV and AIDS patients.

About 600 art therapists are registered with the British Association of Art Therapists, which provides a list of training courses. Both Goldsmiths' College (part of the University of London) and the University of Sheffield provide postgraduate training in art therapy.

Bach Flower Remedies

Dr Edward Bach practised for over 20 years in the UK as a Harley Street consultant, bacteriologist and homoeopath. In 1930 he decided to devote all his time to seeking energies in the plant world which would restore vitality to the sick and prevent disease in the healthy. He considered disease to be the result of conflict between the emotions and emphasised the importance of relaxation and simply 'being'.

Dr Bach claimed that the prevention and cure of disease can take place by ingesting the essences of various herbs, plants and trees. These essences, which he called remedies, harmonise the imbalances of the psyche. The way the individual thinks rather than the nature of the disease is considered paramount. A negative state of mind hinders convalescence and is usually regarded as a primary cause of illness. Thirty-eight basic causes of negative 'states' are said to exist, such as 'fear of worldly things', 'very great hopelessness' and 'no great interest in life', and it is suggested there is very little difficulty in finding the states which exist to determine the necessary remedy or remedies to alleviate the condition.

For information concerning education and training contact the Dr Edward Bach Centre.

Colour Therapy

All animals and plants are affected by changes from light to dark, day to night, and people's attitudes, beliefs and behaviours are greatly influenced by colour.

Various types of colour therapy for disease have been used for thousands of years and the philosophy is rooted in psychological, sensory and parapsychological factors. Egyptian and Greek temples were painted and the choice of colours was thought to be for a deliberate effect. Tibetan teachings recognise the power of colour in meditation. The range of diseases treatable by colour therapy is very extensive and includes migraine, asthma, stress, AIDS, cancer, inflammatory conditions, autism and metabolic problems. High blood pressure may be lowered by the colour blue; conversely, it may be raised by red. Orange helps with depression, while green is associated with soothing nerves and relieving tension. Treatment today uses a light instrument with an appropriate filter to diffuse colour over the whole body or focus it on an affected area.

Further information and details of courses can be obtained from the Hygeia College of Colour Therapy, or from Living Colour.

Dance Therapy

Dance therapy evolved from the theories of Rudolph Laban (1879–1959). The therapy aims to release the natural flow of bodily expression, unique to each individual. Movement is a way of communicating. Dance therapy concentrates on spontaneous, individual movements which emanate from the dancer's experience, not from learning formal dance patterns.

The therapy has proved useful for people who are unable to speak about their feelings, such as autistic children or psychotics. It has also been shown to alleviate anxiety and depression and has helped with illnesses such as schizophrenia, anorexia and bulimia.

Usually sessions take place with a group. The aim is to explore movements and, through the movements, to understand feelings and work out how to deal with them. There are warming up exercises to loosen the muscles. Sometimes there is music to encourage movement, and the therapist may reflect the dancer by mirroring his or her movements, drawing attention to particular gestures, or may invite the dancer to find words for the feelings which emerge.

Dance therapists work in prisons, hospitals, day-care centres, family welfare centres, schools and homes for the elderly, with HIV and AIDS patients, as well as in rehabilitation centres for drug addicts and alcoholics.

The Laban Guild and the Medau Society offer a number of teacher training courses; the University of Hertfordshire provides a postgraduate diploma course in dance therapy.

Hydrotherapy

The originator of hydrotherapy, the therapeutic use of water, was Father Sebastian Kneipp (1821–97). He maintained its purpose was to dissolve and remove impurities and strengthen bodily systems, claiming that water cures every curable disease.

There are many different water therapies. There are hot, cold, neutral, whirlpool and aerated baths. Sitz baths are used for illnesses of the lower abdomen, while sweating baths (the Russian and Turkish varieties) are used to sweat out impurities from the body. Douches, strong streams or sprays of water directed on to the body, stimulate the circulation and ease muscular pain. Colonic irrigation, with water at body temperature being injected into the rectum, is used to clear the colon of poisons, gas, accumulated faecal matter and mucous deposits.

Thalassotherapy utilises the healing powers of sea water or seaweed (but should be avoided by anyone allergic to iodine). Compresses and wraps are used to increase the blood flow to a diseased area for skin disorders, colds, fevers, bronchitis and back pain, while inhalation through the nose of steam vapours from various oils added to hot water helps with coughs or croup.

People with heart disease or high blood pressure should exercise caution before embarking on a course of hydrotherapy.

Iridology

Iridology is based on the pigmentation, structure and markings of an eye's iris which has unique characteristics. These are used to assess the genetic predisposition and tendency towards illness and disease and an evaluation of changes can be recognised using an iris microscope, photography and topography for interpretation. There are three main constitutional types: (a) lymphatic, mainly blue or blue grey in colour with a tendency towards arthritis, rheumatism, catarrh and upper respiratory problems; (b) haematogenous, very dark brown in colour with a tendency towards glandular disturbances and blood disorders; and (c) biliary, a mixture of blue, brown and hazel with a tendency towards diseases of the gall bladder and liver.

The Anglo-European School of Iridology provides a one-year diploma course comprising approximately 700 hours of home study and 150 contact hours, including 20 hours of clinical supervision. Successful passes in the exams allow the trainee practitioner to join the British Society of Iridologists as a Registered Iridologist (RIr).

For further information and details of courses contact the British Society of Iridologists.

Polarity Therapy

This therapy for health and healing was devised by Dr Randolph Stone (1890–1983), who incorporated principles of Eastern and Western healing techniques. He recognised the importance of *Qi* (life energy) which is thought to govern a person's physical, emotional and mental processes. Dr Stone asserted that good health depends upon free-flowing energy and that 'dis-ease' occurs when this energy becomes blocked. Energy flows from a positive to a negative pole, and good health is achieved when it is balanced. In accordance with traditional Indian thinking it is accepted that there are five main *chakras* (centres) from which energy arises – ether, air, fire, water and earth – and that these in turn relate to the various systems and physical parts of the body.

The aim of the therapy is not only to release 'blockages' but also to achieve a balance of the energy currents circulating between these five energy centres, using methods of touch, exercise, diet and awareness skills.

The Polarity Therapy Educational Trust provides a three-year, part-time professional training in all aspects of polarity therapy, and the professional association attached to the Trust is the Polarity Therapy Association. The International School of Polarity Therapy provides a 22-month, part-time (one weekend a month) professional training, and the professional association attached to the School is the International Society of Polarity Therapy.

Radionics

The principles of the alternative therapy of radionics were first discovered by a North American physician, Dr Albert Abrams, early this century. All matter is formed from energy and the human being requires a continuing supply of energy to keep healthy; any interruption in the energy supply through mental, emotional or physical imbalance can lead to a physical dysfunction. Abrams found that he could discover disease in the energy supply system of his patients before the disease manifested as physical symptoms, and with present-day radionic instrumentation it is possible to correct the flow of energy so that either the disease does not materialise in the physical, or if it does, to send corrective energies to regain health. Corrective energies can either be placed in a liquid or tablet, or broadcast in a similar way to the sound and light of television. Radionics can be used for any condition, does not interfere with any other form of treatment and can treat the physical, emotional and mental states of humans, animals, plants and the soil.

A radionic practitioner aims to enhance the natural healing ability of all animals and is concerned with the whole being and total health rather than with just the symptoms of disease. Initial training lasts for three to four years, when the practitioner learns to make a very careful analysis of a patient's health and seeks to establish the causes for any disharmony found. Comprehensive details are obtained about the patient who provides a 'witness', usually in the form of drops of blood or snippets of hair, which act as a link between patient and practitioner as most practitioners analyse and treat from a distance. Subsequently, certain instruments are used to bring the human or other animal back to a balanced state of health by providing energy directly to the site of the disease in question.

Further information about training and organisations can be obtained from The Confederation of Radionic and Radiesthesic Organisations, c/o The Maperton Trust.

Rolfing

The Rolfing method of structural integration, created and developed by Ida Rolf in the 1930s, is a method of deep tissue massage which manipulates the connective tissue (fascia) thereby improving the body's relationship with gravity, easing back, neck and joint pain and helping to resolve unfinished emotional issues which are dramatised in the postural attitudes of the body. It is a powerful massage applied through fingers, knuckles and sometimes elbows.

It is claimed by Rolfers that people function better when they are lined up with gravity and that the human body is so pliable its alignment can be brought into harmony with gravity through manipulation of the connective tissue at almost any time of life. Rolfing eliminates muscle contractions caused by unbalanced structure by lengthening the connective tissue. It improves posture, creates more energy, increases flexibility, coordination and control of the muscles, voice and breath control and makes a person look and feel better, thus positively affecting mood and self concept. Although painful, the pain is always negotiable and only lasts for seconds – the therapy is, after all, about taking trauma out of the body, not putting it in. Rolfing is a set course of treatments comprising 10 sessions working on the whole body, each session building on the one before and each spaced about one week apart.

For further information contact Jennie Crewdson, or the European Rolfing Association.

Shiatsu

Shiatsu, a Japanese word meaning 'finger pressure', is a form of body work which has its roots in TCM. As in acupuncture, shiatsu principles are based on the flow of *Qi* or 'life energy' which circulates through the body in specific channels or meridians. The treatment encourages a steady flow of *Qi*, correcting imbalances so that overall health is increased and many health problems alleviated. Pressure from the thumbs, fingers, palms of the hands, elbows, knees and feet is used in treatment and sometimes gentle stretches are incorporated.

Shiatsu promotes deep relaxation and so can help relieve stress, which is particularly useful in alleviating a wide variety of both acute and chronic conditions. The discipline may also be a means of maintaining health, rather than merely providing a reaction to, or treatment of, an illness. Regular shiatsu sessions are useful as a preventative health measure. In addition to being a therapy shiatsu may also be a means of personal development. Studying the discipline often leads to self-discovery and personal growth.

There are now many schools of shiatsu located throughout the UK, all reputable schools being affiliated to the Shiatsu Society. There are several different styles of shiatsu and different lengths of courses now available. It is worth checking with the Society before undertaking a course of study, especially if studying to practitioner level, as only tuition undertaken with recognised school or teachers counts toward a professional qualification. Schools recognised by the Society follow the Society's teaching guidelines in the form of a core curriculum.

The Shiatsu Society maintains a register of professional practitioners and teachers who are eligible to use the initials MRSS (Member of the Register of the Shiatsu Society). Members recognised as Shiatsu Society practitioners and teachers have undertaken a minimum of three years' training, with recognised schools and teachers, following the core curriculum. This incorporates over 500 hours of formal tuition which includes studying shiatsu techniques and theory along with Western anatomy, physiology and pathology as well as ethics and listening and communication skills. Further information can be obtained from the Shiatsu Society.

14

List of Addresses

Below are listed national and umbrella organisations, training schools and other relevant associations mentioned in the text. Wherever possible phone numbers are included. United Kingdom telephone area codes are due to change on 16 April 1995. Please check any numbers in this book that you plan to use after that date.

National Organisations

British Complementary Medicine Association (BCMA), St Charles Hospital, Exmoor Street, London W10 6DZ; 081-964 1206.

Council for Complementary and Alternative Medicine (CCAM), 179 Gloucester Place, London NW1 6DX; 071-724 9103.

Institute for Complementary Medicine (ICM), PO Box 194, London SW16 1QZ; 071-237 5165.

Research Council for Complementary Medicine, 60 Great Ormond Street, London WC1N 3HR; tel 071-833 8897.

Acupuncture

Council for Acupuncture (*umbrella organisation*), 179 Gloucester Place, London NW1 6DX; 071-724 5756.

British Acupuncture Accreditation Board, 179 Gloucester Place, London NW1 6DX; 071-724 5330.

British Acupuncture Association and Register, 34 Alderney Street, London SW1V 4EU.

British College of Acupuncture, 8 Hunter Street, London WC1N 1BN; 071-833 8164.

Chung San Acupuncture Society, 15 Porchester Gardens, London W2 4DB; 071-229 0136.

College of Traditional Acupuncture UK, Tao House, Queensway, Royal Leamington Spa, Warwickshire CV31 3LZ; 0926 422121.

International College of Oriental Medicine UK, Green Hedges House, Green Hedges Avenue, East Grinstead, West Sussex RH19 1DZ; 0342 313106.

International Register of Oriental Medicine (UK), 4 The Manor House, Colley Lane, Reigate, Surrey RH2 9JW; 0737 242104.

London School of Acupuncture & Traditional Chinese Medicine, Fourth Floor, 60 Bunhill Row, London EC1Y 8QD; 071-490 0513.

Northern College of Acupuncture, 124 Acomb Road, York YO2 4EY; 0904 785120.

Register of Traditional Chinese Medicine, 19 Trinity Road, London N2 8JJ; 081-883 8431.

Traditional Acupuncture Society, 1 The Ridgeway, Stratford-upon-Avon, Warwickshire CV37 9JL; 0789 298798.

Alexander Technique

Society of Teachers of the Alexander Technique (*umbrella organisation*), 20 London House, 266 Fulham Road, London SW10 9EL; 071-351 0828.

Alexander Re-education Centre, 10 Langdon Avenue, Redgrove Meadows, Aylesbury, Buckinghamshire HP21 9UX; 0296 23833.

Alexander Technique Teaching Centre, 63 Chalfont Road, Oxford OX2 6TJ; 0865 58477.

Brighton Alexander Training Centre, 57 Beaconsfield Villas, Brighton, Sussex BN1 6HB; 0273 501612.

Bristol Alexander Technique Training School Association, 37 Bellevue Crescent, Clifton Wood, Bristol BS8 4TF; 0272 298582.

Centre for the Alexander Technique, 46 Stevenage Road, London SW6 6HA; 071-731 6348.

Centre for Training (School Premises), 2nd/3rd Floors, 416 Holloway Road, London N7 6QA; 071-281 7639.

Constructive Teaching Centre Ltd, 18 Lansdowne Road, Holland Park, London W11 3LL; 071-727 7222.

Essex Alexander School, 65 Norfolk Road, Seven Kings, Ilford, Essex IG3 8LJ; 081-598 8247.

Hampstead Alexander Centre, 4 Marty's Yard, Hampstead High Street, London NW3 1QW; 071-435 4840.

North London Teacher-Training Centre, 10 Elmcroft Avenue, London NW11 0RR; 081-455 3938.

North of England Training Centre for the F M Alexander Technique, Flat 3, Park House, 39 Hanover Square, Leeds LS3 1BQ; 0532 449713.

Oxford Alexander Training School, 10 York Road, Headington, Oxford OX3 8NW; 0865 65511.

School of Use, Foxhole, Dartington, Totnes, Devon TQ9 6EB; 0803 201419.

Victoria Training Course for the Alexander Technique, 50a Belgrave Road, London SW1V 1RH; 071-821 7916.

West Sussex Centre for the Alexander Technique, 5 Coates Castle, Near Pulborough, West Sussex RH20 1EU; 0798 82503.

Aromatherapy

Aromatherapy Organisations Council, 3 Latymer Close, Braybrooke, Market Harborough, Leicester LE16 8LN.

Institute of Traditional Herbal Medicine and Aromatherapy, 152c Tufnell Park Road, London N7 0DZ; 071-272 7403.

International Federation of Aromatherapists, Department of Continuing Education, The Royal Masonic Hospital, Ravenscourt Park, London W6 0TN; 081-846 8066.

International Society of Professional Aromatherapists, Hinckley and District Hospital and Health Centre, The Annex, Mount Road, Hinckley, Leicestershire LE10 1AG; 0455 637987.

Register of Qualified Aromatherapists, 52 Barrack Lane, Aldwick, Bognor Regis, West Sussex PO21 4DD; 0243 262035.

School of Holistic Aromatherapy, 108B Haverstock Hill, London NW3 2BD; 071-284 1315.

Shirley Price Aromatherapy Ltd, Essentia House, Upper Bond Street, Hinckley, Leicestershire LE10 1RS; 0455 615466.

The Tisserand Institute, 65 Church Road, Hove, East Sussex BN3 2BD; 0273 206640.

Art Therapy

British Association of Art Therapists, 11a Richmond Road, Brighton, Sussex BN2 3RL.

Goldsmiths' College, University of London, New Cross, London SE14 6NW; 081-692 7171.

University of Sheffield, 16 Claremount Crescent, Sheffield S10 2TA; 0742 768555.

Bach Flower Remedies

The Dr Edward Bach Centre, Mount Vernon, Bakers Lane, Sotwell, Wallingford, Oxfordshire OX10 0PZ; 0491 834678.

Chiropractic

Anglo-European College of Chiropractic, 13–15 Parkwood Road, Bournemouth BH5 2DF; 0202 431021.

British Association for Applied Chiropractic, The Old Post Office, Cherry Street, Stratton Audley, Nr Bicester, Oxfordshire OX6 9BA; 0869 249944.

British Chiropractic Association, 29 Whitley Street, Reading, Berkshire RG2 0EG; (London number) 071-222 8866.

The McTimoney Chiropractic Association (formerly The Institute of Pure Chiropractic), 21 High Street, Eynsham, Oxford OX1 1HE; 0865 880974.

The McTimoney Chiropractic School, 14 Park End Street, Oxford OX1 1HH; 0865 246786.

Witney School of Chiropractic, The Old Post Office, Cherry Street, Stratton Audley, Nr Bicester, Oxfordshire OX6 9BA; 0869 249944.

Colour Therapy

Hygeia College of Colour Therapy, Brook House, Avening, Tetbury, Gloucestershire GL8 8NS; 0453 832150.

Living Colour, 33 Lancaster Grove, Hampstead, London NW3 4EX; 071-794 1571.

Dance Therapy

Laban Guild, c/o Anne Ward, 30 Ringsend Road, Limavady, County Derry, Northern Ireland BT49 0QJ; 0504 762120.

The Medau Society, 8b Robson House, East Street, Epsom, Surrey KT17 1HH; 0372 729056.

University of Hertfordshire, College Lane, Hatfield, Hertfordshire AL10 9PN; 0707 284000.

Herbal Medicine

British Herbal Medicine Association, Field House, Lye Hole Lane, Redhill, Avon BS18 7TB; 0934 862994.

General Council and Register of Consultant Herbalists, 18 Sussex Square, Brighton, East Sussex BN2 5AA; 0273 680504.

National Institute of Medical Herbalists, 9 Palace Gate, Exeter EX1 1JA; 0392 426022.

Register of Chinese Herbal Medicine, PO Box 400, Wembley, Middlesex HA9 9NZ; 081-904 1357.

School of Chinese Herbal Medicine, Midsummer Cottage Clinic, Nether Westcote, Kingham, Oxfordshire OX7 6SD; 0993 830419.

School of Phytotherapy (Herbal Medicine), Bucksteep Manor, Bodle Street Green, Hailsham, East Sussex BN27 4RJ; 0323 833812.

Homoeopathy

Medical Homoeopathy

Faculty of Homoeopathy (*professional umbrella organisation*), The Royal London Homoeopathic Hospital, London WC1N 3HR; 071-837 9469.

British Homoeopathic Association, 27A Devonshire Street, London W1N 1RJ; 071-935 3297.

Homoeopathic Society, Hahnemann House, 2 Powis Place, Great Ormond Street, London WC1N 3HT; 071-837 3297.

Homoeopathic Hospitals

Bristol Homoeopathic Hospital, Cotham Hill, Cotham, Bristol BS6 6JU; 0272 731231.

Glasgow Homoeopathic Hospital, 1000 Great Western Road, Glasgow G12 0NR; 041-339 0382.

Mossley Hill Hospital, Park Hill, Liverpool L18 8BU; 051-250 3000.

The Royal London Homoeopathic Hospital, Great Ormond Street, London WC1N 3HR; 071-837 8833.

Tunbridge Wells Homoeopathic Hospital, Church Road, Tunbridge Wells, Kent TN1 1JU; 0892 542977.

Non-medical Homoeopathy

Society of Homoeopaths (*professional umbrella organisation*), 2 Artizan Road, Northampton NN1 4HU; 0604 21400.

British School of Homoeopathy, 23 Sarum Avenue, Melksham, Wiltshire SN12 6BN; 0225 790051.

College of Classical Homoeopathy, Othergates Clinic, 45 Barrington Street, Tiverton, Devon EX16 6QP; 0884 258143.

College of Homoeopathy, Regent's College, Inner Circle, Regent's Park, London NW1 4NS; 071-487 7416.

College of Practical Homoeopathy (Midlands), 186 Wolverhampton Street, Dudley, West Midlands DY1 3AD; 0384 233664.

London College of Classical Homoeopathy, Morley College, 61 Westminster Bridge Road, London SE1 7HT; 071-928 6199.

London School of Classical Homoeopathy, 1–4 Suffolk Street, London SW1Y 4HG; 0865 331371.

North West College of Homoeopathy, 23 Wilbraham Road, Fallowfield, Manchester M14 6FB; 061-257 2445.

Northern College of Homoeopathic Medicine, First Floor, Swinburne House, Swinburne Street, Gateshead, Tyne and Wear NE8 1AX; 091-490 0276.

Purton House School of Homoeopathy, Purton House, Purton Lane, Farnham Royal, Buckinghamshire SL2 3LY; 0753 646625.

School for Advanced Homoeopathic Studies, 69 West Malvern Road, Worcestershire WR14 4NP; 0684 563192.

School of Homoeopathic Medicine, 29 Manor Street, Otley, West Yorkshire LS21 1AX; 0943 461784.

School of Homoeopathy, Yondercott House, Uffculme, Devon EX15 3DR; 0873 856872.

Yorkshire School of Homoeopathy, Lansdown, 24 Rosebank, Burley-in-Wharfedale, Ilkley, West Yorkshire LS29 7RQ; 0943 863213.

Hypnotherapy

Association of Ethical and Professional Hypnotherapists, 18 The Downs, Harlow, Essex CM20 3RH; 0279 425284.

Association of Hypnotherapy Organisations, 6A Portsmouth Road, Woolston, Southampton SO2 9AM; 0703 438157.

Association of Professional Therapists, 57 The Spinney, Sidcup, Kent DA14 5NE; 081-308 0249.

Central Register of Advanced Hypnotherapists, 28 Finsbury Park Road, London N4 2JX.

National Association of Counsellors, Hypnotherapists and Psychotherapists (and Training Faculty), 145 Coleridge Road, Cambridge CB1 3PN; 0223 247893.

National College of Hypnosis and Psychotherapy, 12 Cross Street, Nelson, Lancashire BB9 7EN; 0282 699378.

National Register of Hypnotherapists and Psychotherapists, 12 Cross Street, Nelson, Lancashire BB9 7EN; 0282 699378.

National School of Hypnosis and Psychotherapy, 28 Finsbury Park Road, London N4 2JX; 071-359 6991.

Proudfoot School of Hypnosis, Blinking Sike, Eastfield Business Park, Scarborough, Yorkshire YO11 3YT; 0723 585960.

Iridology

Anglo-European School of Iridology, 40 Stokewood Road, Bournemouth BH3 7NE; 0202 518078.

British Society of Iridologists, 998 Wimborne Road, Bournemouth, Dorset BH9 2DE; 0202 529793.

Meditation

School of Meditation, 158 Holland Park Avenue, London W11 4UH; 071-603 6116.

Transcendental Meditation, Freepost, London SW1 4YY; 0800 269303.

Naturopathy

General Council and Register of Naturopaths (*umbrella organisation*), Frazer House, 6 Netherhall Gardens, London NW3 5RR; 071-435 8728.

British College of Naturopathy and Osteopathy, Frazer House, 6 Netherhall Gardens, London NW3 5RR; 071-435 6464.

British Naturopathic and Osteopathic Association, BNOA Postgraduate Naturopathic Course, Freepost, Ilminster, Somerset TA19 9BR.

Osteopathy

General Council and Register of Osteopaths (*umbrella organisation*), 56 London Street, Reading, Berkshire RG1 4SQ; 0734 576585.

British College of Naturopathy and Osteopathy, Frazer House, 6 Netherhall Gardens, London NW3 5RR; 071-435 6464.

British School of Osteopathy, 1–4 Suffolk Street, London SW1Y 4HG; 071-930 9254.

European School of Osteopathy, 104 Tonbridge Road, Maidstone, Kent ME16 8SL; 0622 671558.

London College of Osteopathic Medicine, 8–10 Boston Place, London NW1 6QH; 071-262 5250.

Osteopathic Association of Great Britain, 206 Chesterton Road, Cambridge CB4 1NE; 0223 359236.

Osteopathic Information Service, 37 Soho Square, London W1V 5DG; 071-439 7177.

Polarity Therapy

International School and Society of Polarity Therapy, 7 Nunney Close, Golden Valley, Cheltenham, Gloucestershire GL51 0TU; 0242 522352.

Polarity Therapy Educational Trust and Association, 11 The Lea, Allesley Park, Coventry, West Midlands CV5 9HY.

Radionics

The Confederation of Radionic and Radiesthesic Organisations, c/o The Maperton Trust, Wincanton, Somerset BA9 8EH; 0963 32651.

Reflexology

Association of Reflexologists, 130 Harlesden Road, Willesden Green, London NW10 2BB; 081-451 2218.

Bayly School of Reflexology Ltd *and* British Reflexology Association, Monks Orchard, Whitbourne, Hereford and Worcester WR6 5RB; 0886 21207.

British School of Reflexology, The Holistic Healing Centre, 92 Sheering Road, Old Harlow, Essex CM17 0JW; 0279 429060.

Crane School of Reflexology, 135 Collins Meadow, Harlow, Essex CM19 4EJ; 0279 421682.

Lillian Stoltenberg School of Holistic Reflexology and Massage, 27 Haldon Road, Exeter, Devon EX4 4DZ; 0392 219798.

Mary Martin School of Reflexology, 72b Sharps Lane, Ruislip, Middlesex HA4 7JQ; 0895 635621.

Reflexologists' Society, 127 Bullbrook Drive, Bracknell, Berkshire RG12 2QR.

Scottish School of Reflexology and Scottish Institute of Reflexology, 2 Wheatfield Road, Ayr KA7 2XB; 0292 287142.

Rolfing

The Rolf Institute (*international headquarters*), PO Box 1808, Boulder, Colorado 80306-1868, USA.

Jennie Crewdson, 071-834 1493.

European Rolfing Association, Ohmstrasse 9, D–80802, Munich, Germany.

Shiatsu

Shiatsu Society (*umbrella organisation*), 5 Foxcote, Wokingham, Berkshire RG11 3PG; 0734 730836.

Yoga

The British Wheel of Yoga, 1 Hamilton Place, Boston Road, Sleaford, Lincolnshire NG34 7ES; 0529 306851.

Iyengar Yoga Institute, 223a Randolph Avenue, London W9 1NL; 071-624 3080.

Viniyoga Britain, PO Box 158, Bath BA1 2YG; 0225 426327.

Yoga Biomedical Trust, PO Box 140, Cambridge CB4 3SY; 0223 67301; also 60 Great Ormond Street, Royal London Homoeopathic Hospital, London WC1N 3HR; 071-833 7267.

Yoga for Health Foundation, Ickwell Bury, Northill, Biggleswade, Bedfordshire; 0767 627271.

Index